A Dream
of Belonging

My Years in Postwar Poland

JANINA BAUMAN

To Zygmunt

Published by VIRAGO PRESS Limited 1988
41 William IV Street, London WC2N 4DB

Copyright © Janina Bauman 1988

British Library Cataloguing in Publication Data

Bauman, Janina
    A dream of belonging.
    1. Jews, Polish—Europe—Social life
    and customs
    I. Title
    940.55'092'4   DS135.E83

    ISBN 0-86068-975-1

Typeset by Florencetype Ltd. of Kewstoke, Avon
Printed in Great Britain by
Cox & Wyman Ltd. of Reading, Berkshire

Winter struck early in my life. It is autumn now. There have been many springs and summers on the way, and quite a few winters.

I look back puzzled, trying to understand. I want to find a direction in the winding road I took, a hidden logic in what seems, on the surface, a string of unconnected things which 'just happened to me'. Could I have stopped them from happening? And if I could not stop the big things, was it not because I had first allowed the small ones to happen?

I look at the storyteller from the distance of my present age and let her report truthfully what she did and what she thought while doing it. I try not to put into her head thoughts or intentions that, at the time, were not there.

She is a puzzle, that woman, to me. She has brought me here. Let her account for that.

Janina Bauman,
Leeds 1987

All names of the people appearing in this book have been changed, except for those of well-known politicians and film directors.

J.B.

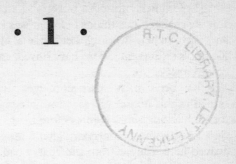

· 1 ·

On Mondays I clean the house. Wearing old trousers and a one-time best blouse, armed with rags and brushes, detergents and sprays, I launch the offensive first thing in the morning. The kitchen is small but always a jumble, however hard I try to keep it tidy. By the time I've done the cupboards, cooker, and window-sill, I feel I'm halfway through. The breakfast-room is messy too. We eat here, but Konrad also uses it as his workshop, along with the larder that serves him as a darkroom and the studio upstairs that used to be Sylvia's room. Odd prints, often spread on the sideboard to dry, cookery books, maps and travel guides, piles of letters and bills waiting to be answered, seven huge jars of home-made wine, Konrad's pride and joy – all these crowd the breakfast-room and need my constant attention. Then 'the salon', a much-used room where we sit together to talk, drink, read, listen to music or watch television. The books here need dusting, like others all over the house. When I have finished the hall with its grandfather clock and my home-made pots that gather so much dust, I've usually had enough. I skip the study and seldom bother with the dining-room which only needs tidying after a dinner party. Not very often, that is. I may leave the upper floor for another day. It doesn't need much cleaning, now that there are only the two of us left in this big house.

Sometimes the house seems far too big for us. Too big to be kept warm and tidy. Why do we need such a huge place, we've been asking ourselves, since the girls have left home and my mother has died? Once we decided to sell it and buy something small. We quickly found a buyer and a contract was drawn up. But we changed our minds before it was signed: why move if we are happy where we are? Let's stay a little longer, at least till Konrad's retirement. So we have stayed, and this makes me happy day after day.

It has been many years since we came to this country and settled in this house. Never before have I lived in the same place for such a long time. Never before have I owned a house. When on a hot summer's afternoon, after a long drive from Dover, we arrived here straight from the boat, I could hardly believe it was ours: the big garden brimming with roses, lilies, forget-me-nots and dandelions; the two ancient trees – an oak and a beech – casting their long shadows over the tangled lawn; the forlorn greenhouse full of broken pots, rusty tools, leaky watering-cans; the ramshackle wooden garage, swathed by a climbing rose in full bloom, and piled high inside with lumber accumulated, no doubt, by generations of successive owners.

Then the house itself. Late afternoon light sifted through the stained-glass panels of the windows, and lay in coloured shapes on the well-worn carpets in the empty rooms. The murky hall, the staircase, the threadbare bedrooms shamelessly displayed in the last beams of sunset, every corner, every recess told tales of someone's past life, which, for one reason or another, had had to be halted and continued elsewhere. There was a sense of mystery around, lurking in the rooms, lingering in the garden. Spell-bound, we wandered, up and down, touching the walls in disbelief. An intimation of time to come, a faint hope for the future crept into my timid heart.

'An Englishman's home is his castle.' I shall never be English or pretend I am. 'Be always what you are, never pretend you're someone else,' my father used to say when I was a child. Here I would lock myself in to live a secluded family life and remain for ever a stranger to the outer world. May this old English house become a stranger's castle. I hoped it would be spacious enough to house my memories.

An elderly couple turned up at the gate – the neighbours from the opposite house. They had heard we were coming long before, and had seen us arrive. Could they be of any help? They would be only too happy to show us around, lend us pots and pans and anything else we might need until we'd settled down. The old lady tottered back to fetch a bottle of milk and some sweets for the girls. Then, as we started unloading the car, a young woman, another neighbour, came to introduce herself and invited us to tea. We were all smiles, too shy and too tired to accept the invitation. Not till the following day did I pluck up the courage to call on our neighbours to thank them for their welcome. 'I'm so graceful,' I told the elderly couple. The old gentleman smiled: 'Graceful you are indeed, and there's no need to be grateful.'

I remember this first day of our life in Britain in minute details. It was Friday. Konrad went off to the university early in the morning to stay there till evening. It was nearly the end of term and he had a lot to do before the start of the summer holidays. So there we were, the twins and myself, alone in the house, labouring to turn it into a home. The day was bright, beaming with sunlight, warbling with birdsong. Where was the notorious British smog, the Dickensian gloom? We started work in earnest, scrubbing, dusting, sweeping the cobwebs away. What was left of the old furniture and possessions had to be sorted out, thrown away, or cleaned and stored to make room for our own belongings that were soon to arrive. The telephone was dead, but from his office Konrad urged the shops to send in as soon as possible a few things that we had ordered in advance. As the morning wore on, the beds arrived, a table and chairs, a cooker. The house swarmed with men carrying furniture, fixing pipes, smiling at us in a friendly way and speaking broad Yorkshire. It was beyond my understanding and, crestfallen, I hardly dared open my mouth. Only then did I realise how much Sylvia had learnt from her English lessons in Warsaw. The shy one, the quieter of the twins, always a little withdrawn and subdued, she suddenly took over the task of talking to the men. She told them that we could only understand if they spoke slowly and clearly. So, when after a time I asked whether they would care for a cup of tea or coffee, one lad with smiling eyes, prodding at his and his mate's chests with his forefinger, shouted out loud, as if I were deaf and mentally deficient: 'Me tea, he coffee.' However, as we sipped our drinks together, we embarked upon a conversation exchanging details about our names and places of birth.

At noon I made a bold decision to go out and do some shopping. The small supply of food we had bought on the motorway a day before was now nearly finished. I couldn't persuade either of the girls to come with me: carried away with teenage zeal they were happily weeding the garden under the blazing sky. A little transistor radio, hidden in the tall grass, roared with catchy songs that only some time later I came to identify as Top of the Pops from the early 70s. 'The night is dark, the day is bright,' proclaimed a vigorous male voice, over and over again. And whenever I remember the first day of my life here, this voice, this simple tune always comes back to me.

There are no local shops in our neighbourhood. The nearest shopping centre is twelve minutes' walk away. Spoiled by the closeness of all those little shops that in Warsaw and Tel-Aviv thrive at the feet of big apartment houses, I found it a major problem.

First time alone on British soil I walked through our quiet suburb, dying for fear lest I should be suddenly spoken to by a stranger. But at this time of the day there were very few people about and nobody spoke to me – only two or three old ladies smiled gently as they passed by. This was new and I liked it: strangers do not smile at each other in Warsaw or Tel Aviv. Later I learned it was a Yorkshire habit, one of those that make me feel more comfortable here.

From the three shops in the little centre I chose the Co-op because it was self-service: I hoped I would not need to speak. In vain. The woman at the till beamed with such broad friendliness that I felt obliged to say something. So I introduced myself as a new customer coming straight from overseas and badly needing her help. She seemed overjoyed and instantly left the till to show me round. 'First thing you have to learn, luv,' she shouted, 'is decimalisation. A pound has 100 pennies now and there are no shillings. It's a bit hard to learn and nobody likes it. But don't worry luv, you'll get used to it.' Silently blessing the pound's decimalisation, I desperately tried to make the lbs and the ozs into kilograms and grammes, while the friendly cashier stared at me bewildered and helpless.

When in the evening, tired and excited, Konrad came home after his first long day at his new job, he found the house already turned into something that vaguely resembled a home. The brand-new round table in the breakfast room was laid for supper, sheets of paper serving as plates, a single spoon, a knife and a fork to be shared by the four of us. We had only just begun to wonder whether we liked the unfamiliar taste of ready-made pork pies, when an abrupt knocking at the back door made us jump to our feet.

Since the years that I spent as a young girl hiding in occupied Warsaw, I have always been deadly scared of sudden knocking. When in March 1968 we expected Konrad to be arrested any time, the slightest rustle behind the front door of our Warsaw flat would make my blood freeze. Now, in this safe remote country, in this quiet friendly house, I felt my heart go still again.

A stranger, a sullen-looking man in his forties entered the room, greeting us in English. He introduced himself as a member of the Anglo-Polish Society, then switched into rusty Polish to say that he had heard rumours about a Polish scholar settling in the town, found the address, and was calling to see whether we needed his help. He sat down sulkily at our new table, not knowing what to say next, or possibly shy because of his awkward Polish. We kept an apprehensive silence, too. The stranger stared at the half-eaten scraps and greasy sheets littering the table, and this made us feel even more uneasy. After a while he left, bidding us good luck and promising to call again. As the door banged after him, we looked anxiously at each other. Who was this stranger and what did he really want? During the last three years in Israel we had almost forgotten our earlier fear. Now it came back in a flash. Had we been followed again? Was the mighty U.B.* able to reach as far as the British Isles? Poor old Jan has never known what a panic he caused on his first surprise visit. It

* U.B. – internal security: Polish equivalent of Russian K.G.B.

was a long time before we learned to trust him and see a good reliable friend in this Polish ex-serviceman, British scientist, and weather-beaten climber of the Yorkshire hills.

Whenever I finish my Monday housework and can at last think of something else, I take a short break and, with a cup of strong black coffee and a cigarette, start wandering about the house. It feels so peaceful, so snug. The branches of the old trees swing in the wind outside the bay-windows; the rooms bask in sun or if it is raining drowse in greenish shades. The sweet tunes of Chopin, or Mozart or Bach flow from Radio Three. The grandfather clock ticks gently away, bringing me closer to the time when I shall see Konrad again.

I have grown to love this house as though it were a person I do not wish to part from. I have never known such a feeling before. Perhaps because the innumerable places I have lived in throughout my long life have not really been mine, or were too small or far less private. Or maybe because I was never satisfied with myself, though happy more often than not, during those long years. Or for the obvious reason that my earlier life was so busy and full that my home was never of paramount importance. Quite often these days, in my hospitable English house, I sink back into memories of those earlier places, recalling moments, chapters and decades in my earlier life. Not that I really feel old, or close to a final departure, or that my present time is empty: in my late fifties and in good health, free at last from both maternal and professional duties, I have many good reasons to be thankful for my life. Yet, at this stage of the road one tends to look back, to compare and draw conclusions. The past brought forth to the present day seems to shed a new light on the 'now' and 'here'; it adds a deeper meaning to the present and helps to guide me through what is still left ahead.

I can recapture all my life by calling to mind, one by one, all the rooms, flats and houses I have lived in.

My early childhood . . .

. . . A colourful frieze runs along the top of the nursery walls, round and round the room. Over and over again, it shows the same two children playing with the same dog. Everybody is still fast asleep in the villa, a cuckoo calls somewhere . . . Our ancient gardener is already up digging the flower-beds: tap, tap goes the spade against the fresh soil. He won't see me if I steal through behind his bent back.

. . . Quickly, softly, barefoot in my nightie, I tiptoe down the stairs shivering from excitement and from the morning chill; quick, quick across the roomy hall lest grandfather sees me here, straight to the front door. The key rasps in the lock, once, twice, it works, it works . . . the hinges creak . . . the first rays of the rising sun briefly dazzle my eyes.

. . . The bright cool gravel of the garden path pricks my bare feet. There is a smell of freshness in the air, a bitter scent of soil, of dew, of a distant forest. I am alone on the garden path and feel a little guilty, and thrilled, and joyous. It must be happiness, but I don't know that yet.

. . . The same garden path, the same villa, but now I am eighteen. We return here in tatters, having nowhere else to go. 'We' now means Mother, Sophie and myself – all our loved ones have been killed in the war or are wandering somewhere in the world. Our pre-war Warsaw home was ruined years before and this old summer house is the only place we hoped to find untouched. Untouched it is, but there is no room for us – it now belongs to the Polish Army and is being used as a hospital. The old gardener and his wife have luckily survived. They take us to their cottage, next to the garage. Here we stay, exhausted and half-starved, sharing the old couple's humble meals, until a kind doctor, an old friend of my father's, takes pity on us and offers us a shelter in his luxurious villa.

*

Whenever I can spare a little time, I settle down cosily in the study to do a bit of writing. This is what I most like doing. In my busy life, in crowded flats, I could seldom find time and peace to write just for pleasure. Only when I retired and suddenly found myself alone in this spacious house, with no urgent duties and no noble cause ahead, free at last to do what I had always wanted, have I taken to writing in earnest and can never stop. Here memories flow freely back and form the basis of my stories. Struggling with the English language that has become mine far too late in life, I write one story after another and send them off to popular magazines. No success so far.

One of my recent stories draws on that short but bitter spell in the kind doctor's luxurious villa. It takes place in late July 1945. Warsaw lies in ruins. Survivors returning from their war-wanderings settle in a once-elegant suburb that has luckily escaped bombings and fire. The local secondary school has opened and pupils spend long hours there to make up for the time they have lost.

One warm evening Helena and Tom leave school together and walk through the suburb towards Helena's home.

The stately roof of the villa had just emerged from behind the poplar trees, when the girl stopped. If they walked on any further, she thought, she would have to invite Tom for tea. They had recently become good friends and she wondered why Tom never asked her to come to his home. On the other hand, she did not want to invite him to hers – and she had a good reason not to. She couldn't possibly let him see her squalid little room in the dark, damp basement of this magnificent villa which belonged to a rich doctor, a friend of her dead father from before the war. No, Helena couldn't let Tom see how poor she and her mother were, how humiliated by the doctor's kindness; and how lonely, with all their relatives lost in the holocaust. She knew Tom's family had survived the war in their suburban mansion – nobody had been killed. And they were fairly well off, since Tom's father owned a small factory which had never stopped working, even during the German occupation. In fact, there were many pupils at school who seemed to live quite comfortably: they wore proper clothes and didn't look half-starved. As for Helena, she felt hungry from early morning till late night. Her only dress was awkwardly sewn by her mother from an old linen curtain which the kind doctor had given them. It didn't matter so much now that it was summer: Helena knew that sunburnt, slim and with an abundance of dark hair and bright green eyes, she was still an attractive girl, despite her worn shoes and horrid school bag. Yes, they were poor, Mother and herself, but far from self-pitying. They hoped for a better future when Mama would find a job, and for a better one still when Helena could go to work. It was not far away: she was eighteen and working hard to make up for the long gap in her studies. In a year she should be ready to leave school with a good certificate. And then . . . For the time being, though, they had to live on UNRRA parcels. This was one more thing she didn't want Tom to know.

Now it's time for Helena and Tom to say goodbye to each other, and time for me, the author, to say something that I hope will please the readers of a popular magazine.

Helena didn't feel ready to part with Tom just yet. How sweet, how reassuring it was to walk arm in arm with this subtle, intelligent boy on that fragrant evening; to talk to him and listen to his deep voice, to feel his fair, gentle face so close to hers. If only it could last, if only he would stay close till the end of this final school year. Or perhaps longer . . . She wouldn't feel lonely any more, there would be someone to share thoughts with, to enjoy freedom together, to laugh and brood, work and play – or perhaps just sit still in silence holding hands.

Tom didn't seem to want to say goodbye either. Without a word, they turned to the left, leaving the villa behind them. Soon, they were walking along a deserted railway track that ran to nowhere through the thick forest.

Here comes the most romantic bit: they feel as though there's just the two of them in the whole world, no other human being on this abandoned railway track; the sunset paints their way with fire; birds go crazy with their goodnight songs. Suddenly something rustles in the bushes and on a mutual impulse they clasp each other. A long, long kiss . . .

This should do. Now switch to the fast moving action:

Suddenly she felt Tom's arms fall apart. She opened her eyes. A man on horseback was riding towards them.

'He must have seen us,' she whispered.

Still pale and moved, Tom smiled gently at her: 'Does it matter, Helena?'

As the man came closer, they saw he was a Russian soldier. There were lots of Russian soldiers around – a large military unit had its quarters in the suburb. Most people hated them, some feared them. Not Helena, though: they had liberated the South of Poland just in time to save her life. Besides, they protected the poor against the rich. Helena was poor, she hated the rich. She gave a friendly smile to the approaching man.

Tom's face contracted when he saw the soldier, his teeth clenched. Oh, he hated them with all his heart, the damned Bolsheviks. Hadn't they lain in wait on the opposite side of the river last September when the Warsaw insurgents were bleeding to death in their hopeless battle against the Nazis? Hadn't they rejoiced in the defeat of the heroes and the carnage that had followed instead of rushing to help? Tom hadn't been in the fight, his parents wouldn't let him go, he had stayed safe in his mansion. But many of his teenage friends had fought. Some of them had been killed. The very sight of Russians who hadn't given a damn for young Polish lives was loathsome to Tom.

The man grinned in a familiar way as he approached. He muttered a greeting in Russian. He had the broad, red face of a Russian peasant, and cunning little eyes. He was clearly drunk. He stopped, climbed down from his horse, and pulled out of his breast-pocket a flat bottle of vodka. *'Pieite tovarischi na zdarove,'* he mumbled, pointing the bottle at Tom; then in clumsy Polish he repeated: 'Have a nice gulp, comrades.'

Tom jerked back, his teeth clenched, unable to utter a word. Helena felt uneasy. Plucking up her courage, she said firmly:

'It's kind of you, comrade, but we don't like vodka. Besides, we have to go now.' She made a move to pass but the man laughed and suddenly grasped her arm.

'Wait, wait little girl. Don't like vodka – mustn't drink. Come on, mount the horse, have a nice ride instead.'

'Leave her in peace, will you!' shrieked Tom in fury. Fiercely he pulled Helena's arm from the stranger's grip. 'Come on!' he commanded sharply. Off they went, leaving the puzzled man behind. They strode, almost ran along the track, not looking back, not uttering a word. Soon they heard the clatter of hooves. Here they were again, the horse and its master.

'Listen boy,' the drunken man said, trying to slow down and keep to their pace, 'let that girl have a ride with me. I fancy her. In ten minutes' time you'll have her back.'

In desperate resolution Tom seized Helena's hand and dragged her into the forest. Now they were madly running away, straight through the bushes, deep into the shadow of the trees.

'What if he finds us here?' whispered Helena, seized with terror.

'I know what I'm doing,' hissed Tom in reply. 'Just follow me.'

They had left the track far behind when, all of a sudden, the forest grew thinner and the red light of the sunset emerged from behind the trees. They had reached the edge of the wood and stopped, gasping for breath. And here he finally caught up with them, the sweating, panting, bewildered man.

All his friendliness had gone. 'Look, you bastard,' he shouted, 'look what I'm going to do to your girl. Watch and learn from me, you damned kid!' He jumped down from the horse and was just about to grab Helena when Tom intervened. Nimble, fast, precise and in the nick of time

· 11 ·

he pulled the girl away from the soldier, facing him with a clenched fist.

The drunken man jerked back, staggered. With a hideous Russian curse he grasped his gun, his finger on the trigger. But Tom was faster. Jerking up the hand that held the weapon, he pressed the man's finger down. With an ear-splitting burst the gun fired into the darkening sky.

'Lie down!' commanded Tom, and Helena dropped flat to the grass.

'Help!' screamed Tom. 'Dad, Mum, help me! He's killed the girl, he's shot her dead!'

In utmost terror the soldier managed to climb onto his horse. The clatter of the hooves died away and it was the last sound they heard from him.

And so anti-climax.

For a long while Helena lay still on the ground, unable to move. Terror, shame and an endless gratitude to Tom, mixed with boundless admiration, took hold of her. Slowly, reluctantly and not looking at her, the boy started off towards the mansion that could be clearly seen at the edge of the forest. Helena stood up and followed him. They were approaching Tom's home.

Alarmed by the shot and Tom's cries, a group of people were running from the house to meet them. Tom's parents, it seemed, servants and relatives. They reached Tom, seized him and in a confusion of hugs and kisses stormed him with questions. With the danger now gone, he collapsed into his mother's arms. Horrified, Helena watched Tom sobbing like a child as they took him home.

It was his home, his family whom I didn't know. I was too shy to follow without an invitation. So I stayed behind.

Entirely forgotten, she was left on her own at the entrance to the mansion garden. Her legs gave way, she sat down on the graveled drive, leaning against the gate. She felt exhausted and ravenous. Her arms and legs were scratched, her home-made dress torn. She closed her eyes.

Soon, she heard the sounds of people settling down for a meal on the verandah. A divine smell of food reached her nostrils. Then all sounds and smells died away: Helena was falling asleep.

At last, conclusion of the story with a twist in the tale.

When she opened her eyes again, a well-groomed middle-aged lady was walking towards her with a kindly smile. Helena recognised Tom's mother and tried to smile back. 'Hallo, Helena,' said the lady. 'I'm so sorry we meet in these most unpleasant circumstances, but would you, please . . .' She suddenly paused, taken aback, and gave the girl a sharp look. 'Listen, child,' she said curtly. 'You'd better sit for a moment on the bench and calm down. When we finish our dinner, my husband will drive you home.' And off she went.

Helena lifted herself from the ground. Struggling to overcome a new wave of terror, she plunged back into the dark forest on her lonely way home.

The Editor thanks you for submitting the enclosed MS but regrets that it is not suitable for our publication.

A handwritten postscript – 'Keep trying!' – is apparently meant to encourage my further attempts. But I do not need encouragement: once I have started, I will go on with my stories until death alone parts me from the typewriter.

I know the story is unclear. 'Why,' the editor might ask, 'did Tom's mother change her mind and tell Helena to wait on the bench instead of inviting her to dinner?' The point is that the girl looks Jewish. She *is* Jewish, beyond any doubt. Just because Tom's mother recoils from inviting her in and encouraging her friendship with her son, it does not mean that she is anti-Semitic. Nonetheless, Jews who have survived the hell of the holocaust are unwelcome. They are somehow soiled, marked with suffering, branded with tragedy. It is better to keep away from them and not let the evil taint one's own tidy life.

This wouldn't be clear to the editor of a British magazine or to anyone who never lived in Poland at the end of the war. It is not clear even to myself, though I was there and went through it all. Not just the episode described in this story – all my life story must seem confused and ambiguous to strangers, as it is to myself. It was – it is – because I was – I am – Jewish.

Somehow it was easier to know where you were under the German occupation. There were the Nazis intent upon killing all Jews and many Poles. There were the Jews, doomed to die. There were the Poles who lived in constant terror and who either helped the Jews, or threatened them, or turned a blind eye on the Jewish ordeal, out of fear and sometimes, maybe, for less understandable reasons. Now, after the war, this all suddenly got muddled up. The Nazis were gone, the pattern was shattered. The Poles and the Jewish wrecks were left on their own in their devastated country. The terror was over but the memories remained. It was hard for the Poles, I think, to see Jewish survivors as just their compatriots. They reminded them of something they would have rather forgotten. Sometimes – maybe – of a guilty conscience.

That we were unwanted became obvious to me very soon after the liberation. But I couldn't then understand why. So I lived in total confusion.

· 2 ·

During the first years after the war I wanted to leave Poland – to get away from a place where I was seen as an unwanted stranger. I felt lonely at school, lonely among my neighbours, singled out and set apart in the very place where I felt I belonged.

Things changed little when we had left Konstancin, the stiff-upper-lip suburb, and moved to Warsaw. It happened in September 1945. A friend turned up and suggested we share a flat with him. He was over seventy and, like ourselves, had survived the holocaust. Straight after the war he had married a widow less than half his age. They had money and friends in the right places and had managed to find an empty flat in one of the very few big houses in the ruined capital that had miraculously escaped devastation. There was a terrible shortage of living space in Warsaw, so there was no question of Mr and Mrs Lark keeping the whole flat to themselves. Anxious they might be forced to share it with a family of ten, they turned to us instead. We gladly accepted the offer and moved to our new home.

It was, in fact, a single room, very small and very dark; it was on the sixth floor and from its window we looked down into the courtyard, a dreary well. We were allowed to use the bathroom next to our room. The toilet was at the other end of the flat, so we had to walk through the Larks' room every time we wanted to use it, while they walked through ours whenever they needed a bath. The kitchen belonged to them and we had no access to it. We had an electric plate on our bedside table and that was our kitchen.

All the same we were happy while the Larks remained friendly. But that very soon changed. Mr Lark turned out to be a dreadful old man, nosy, malicious, and ill-tempered. Throughout all those long years we had to live with him he was a constant source of trouble to us.

My mother, who had never worked before but knew four foreign languages, immediately found an office job. She earned far too little, however, to support all three of us. It was why my sister Sophie, now fifteen, made the brave offer to live in a children's home. She was promptly admitted to a Jewish war-orphans' home (which also accepted half-orphans) and left us, to live and go to school in Sosnowo, a little health resort near Warsaw. At the same time I enrolled in an evening school for adults. It was to be the last year of my schooling and with finals coming up the following June, I had to work extremely hard. My days were now filled to the brim with homework and with the coaching that I gave to backward children in order to make up our slender income. I spent my evenings at school, among strangers that I never managed to make friends with.

It was a hard, sad time. Our faint hope that Father might still be alive was shattered when the International Red Cross con-firmed his death in the Katyn Forest in Russia. We still believed that the Nazis had been responsible for this mass slaughter. Thousands of people who had fled from the approaching Ger-mans at the outbreak of war had taken refuge in Russia. Now they were surging back. My mother's brother, Uncle Jerzy, returned from the Soviet Union as an officer in the new Polish army. His wife and little daughter had found shelter in a Russian-occupied town in the East of Poland, but were later murdered when the Nazis took over the town. After a time Uncle Jerzy had remarried and now brought with him a lovely Russian wife who, like himself, was a military doctor and a major. All plump and round, her exuberant breasts raised to her chin by her tight uniform, she told us she was pregnant. New life was springing up from the ruins of the past.

Only a few of my friends had survived. It was hard to revive our previous intimacy; each of us had a different story of survival behind her and different aims or hopes ahead. The boy who I had once been in love with in the dark days of the ghetto, had also escaped death. We met in the street by chance soon after my return to Warsaw. But he had changed. Blond and blue-eyed, he took great care not to be identified as a Jew. He kept his false surname which had helped him to survive the occupation and was reluctant to introduce me to his new friends in case they might guess his secret. To me it was shameful, more than I could forgive. I lost my respect for him and with that, my love.

My desire to leave Poland now grew stronger than ever before. Having dreamt for years of a full, useful life, I did not know how to anchor my dreams in the world around me. Things were happening fast. Warsaw was returning to life at a tremendous speed. The new government, the workers' party, called on everyone to fight for reconstruction and a new social deal. I was not opposed to this, I strongly approved, but I held myself aloof: somehow the slogans seemed too obtrusive, the posters too crude, the cheers too loud. Among the few Party members I came to know, there seemed to be no-one I could fully trust or respect: most of them, I suspected, were just after an easy career. The ones who sounded honest, the old communists who before the war had rotted in jail for their beliefs, showed such a fierce intolerance for those they called 'class enemies' that I could hardly imagine myself thinking and acting like them. I decided to emigrate.

Haunted by dreadful memories, many Jewish survivors were leaving for Palestine. It was a dangerous business – both leaving Poland and entering Palestine were illegal. Yet they kept trying. Usually they ended up in the refugee camps in Western Europe and stayed there for a long time before they finally managed to reach their destination. In March 1946 a friend introduced me to a Zionist organisation.

About Zionism I knew as little as about Communism, or even less. I certainly had no idea that there were different streams within the movement itself. 'Going to Palestine' had for me a rather simple meaning: sacrificing one's life in order to build a home for the homeless Jews of the world by making barren deserts into lush gardens and teeming new towns. And this I was ready to do.

I went to a shabby place on the outskirts of Warsaw to meet the 'manager'. A matter-of-fact young man briefly explained to me the aims of the organisation. Any young Jewish man or woman who wanted to live in Palestine was welcome, no matter what their social background or beliefs might be. The members lived together, forming a little commune called a *kvutza*. Their task was to learn Hebrew and to prepare themselves for the hardships of rural life in a kibbutz. There were already about twenty people living upstairs, the man said, and I was welcome to join them. I would have to start at once, however, in two or three days at the most, because the *kvutza* was leaving at the end of April and there was very little time left for me to learn some Hebrew and the essentials of collective life. As he spoke, I decided in a sudden flash of resolution to join the strangers and to leave my country, my family, my studies. This was the way to be useful, to belong somewhere, to live for a clear-cut purpose. It was this that I had longed for throughout the endless years of the war while trapped in the Warsaw ghetto and later when hiding, running away, wasting days one after another. I said yes.

Three days later I joined the *kvutza*. Mother did not object too strongly: she knew how I felt, she felt the same. One of us had to take the first step. But she was terribly worried about my studies. There were only three months left to the finals. Why not wait till I got my certificate? I would not listen. A document confirming my high school graduation was the last thing I would need to turn the desert into a fertile field. Sophie sent her blessing. She belonged to a secret Zionist group in her home and was planning to leave for Palestine. We would soon meet there.

The *kvutza* occupied two seedy rooms with a tiny kitchen above the manager's office. One room for girls, one for boys. We slept on wooden bunks ranged on the three levels round the walls. We had to use a wooden privy in the courtyard and to wash in cold water in a shared wash-basin. All daily chores were shared: each day three couples were on duty, cooking, cleaning and washing. All members of the commune also had their special duties. I was put in charge of laundry, which meant supervising the work of those who did the washing and allocating clean sheets, towels and clothes – clothes were shared too. We spent our days studying. One of the members taught Hebrew. The manager taught everything else. We studied the history of the Jews and elementary agriculture; we read writings by the fathers of Zionism, sang Hebrew songs and rehearsed the principles of collective life. The educational background of most of the students was poor; some had not even completed primary school. Very soon the manager asked me to prepare a series of talks on wider subjects, such as the invention of print or the Industrial Revolution. I was exempted from cooking and cleaning and allowed to spend some time in the public library. I had to admit I liked it better this way. On the other hand, it made me feel uneasy: I felt singled out yet again.

It was not long before I realised that my old dream of belonging had not come true. My fellow-members were not what I had hoped they would be. They came from all walks of life, some from God-forsaken little places – their first time in a big city. They had little in common with each other – but for one thing: like myself, they all had gone through horrifying experiences during the war, had lost their families and had joined the *kvutza* mainly to escape from loneliness. Only a few were truly committed to the Zionist idea and ready for sacrifice. The rest could not care less. All they longed for was to leave the country where their loved ones had been murdered. There were also some – two or three – who hoped that in the West, no matter where, they could become rich. My disappointment grew from day to day. Gradually I was coming to the conclusion that I made a serious mistake in joining the *kvutza*. But the very thought of withdrawing seemed degrading.

Various boys and girls in the *kvutza* were getting together and forming couples. There was no one around I wanted as my boy-friend, but there was someone I was fond of. A dark, strong, thoughtful man in his late twenties, Fred felt out of place – much like myself. And he respected me more than anyone else. We became friends and talked a lot about our future. Fred's memories were sombre. He had lost all his family during the war and had gone through a terrible ordeal, hiding alone in a deserted graveyard for nine months. He was not a Zionist. His only wish was to leave Poland and to try to live somewhere else, never to look at the graves again. He strongly disapproved of my decision to join the *kvutza* and leave my mother and sister behind. He kept saying I did not belong here and should go back to my mother. Deep in my heart I knew he was right but would not admit it even to myself.

The date for the departure of the *kvutza* was coming closer. It was scheduled for 30 April. On 21 April I was taken ill. I lay numb on my bunk just below the ceiling, dazed by a splitting headache and high fever, unable to move or think. Excited by the forthcoming journey and busy with preparations, my fellow travellers paid me little attention. All except Fred who was there, ready to help. Asking no one's permission, he took me in his strong arms, carried me downstairs, put me on a tram and took me straight to my mother's. There, in our dark little room, I spent three weeks with measles which, having come late in my life, was particularly severe. Meantime the *kvutza* left. Fred stayed behind. He found himself somewhere to live and kept in touch with me for a year. Then he left Poland and my life.

I recovered at the end of May and went back to school. The final exams were to start the following week. The headmaster told me I could sit them if I felt I still had a chance. I did this and, despite all odds, passed the whole lot by the skin of my teeth.

Soon after collecting the miserable certificate, I fell ill again. This time it was TB which I had contracted during the war – the measles had stirred it up again. Bedridden and raving with fever, I half-dreamed of a desert under a blazing sun and of slender palm-trees reaching for a cloudless sky. These images would run away from me till they became distant and blurred. Then they would return. I was sent to a sanatorium.

The sanatorium nestled in the woods of Otwock, a health resort near Warsaw, only two miles away from where Sophie was living. My recovery was fast: the fresh, dry air of the pine woods, the substantial meals, the peacefulness of the place were all I really needed. After a week I was able to get up and spend most of the day in the open stretched out on a deck-chair in the sanatorium's park. There were many other patients resting in the park. They welcomed me as if I were a new member of their club. In fact, they did form a club of a kind. Men and women of all ages and from various walks of life, they all had something in common: TB. Moreover, they all stood a good chance of recovery. The seriously ill patients, those who were infectious therefore dangerous, lived in a separate wing of the building and rested in another corner of the park. So it was 'them' and 'us' and, unexpectedly, I found what I had always looked for, the joy of belonging. Very soon I became deeply involved in the daily life of the sanatorium, keen to know all about the health and the lives of my fellow patients, and gladly telling them my own stories. I played cards, read and discussed books, and also edited a satirical news bulletin which aimed to play down the misery of our passive existence. Many friendships sprang up among the patients, love affairs and betrayals, scandals and fits of jealousy. Two fellow patients proposed to me – one in his forties, the other my age. Both were rejected, though I liked them both.

I now had plenty of time to think about my future and what I would do when I left the sanatorium. My resolution to leave Poland was stronger than ever: the terrifying news of the pogrom in Kielce* enflamed old wounds and made the matter urgent. I told myself again and again that I had to leave for Palestine. But then I calmed down: it had to take time, I had to find the right way. How to do it? I didn't know. Joining another *kvutza* was out of the question. On the other hand, I desperately wanted to study. With my brand-new certificate, however paltry it might be, I was entitled to apply to the university. But to study what? My father had always wanted me to be a doctor like himself, like my

---

* On 4 July 1946 in Kielce, a small community of Jews who had recently settled in this provincial town, was suddenly attacked by a raging crowd, accused of having committed a ritual murder. Present-day historians believe that the pogrom was due to provocation but still do not know who was to blame. The fact is that on that day forty-two Jewish holocaust survivors were killed by their Polish neighbours.

grandfather and like most of my uncles. I had always taken it for granted that would be what I would do. But now, in the sanatorium, I suddenly realised that I had no wish to be a doctor. There was one thing I liked more than anything else: writing. I decided to study journalism.

There were two major obstacles, however. First, in order to study I had to find a job to support myself. Secondly, journalism seemed incompatible with my long-range plan to emigrate to Palestine: what would a Polish journalist do with her perfect Polish style in a Hebrew-speaking country?

The only person with whom I could share my hopes and doubts was Mother. Left on her own and feeling lonely, she would travel to spend a few hours with Sophie or with me on Sundays. Although my resolution to give up medical studies was a great disappointment for her, she did not object, strongly believing that whatever decision I made would be the best. Yet, neither of us knew what exactly I should do when I left the sanatorium.

Unexpectedly this question was answered by someone else, or rather the answer was made less urgent. The doctor said I was almost cured but could only be discharged from the sanatorium on condition I stayed in the country, for at least the following winter. My sister Sophie once again came up with a good idea: her children's home was in desperate need of a coach to help the eldest group catch up at secondary school. She had a word with the director and on the following day he sent me an invitation for an interview. I walked two miles, saw the director and his wife, spoke with them for half an hour and was offered the job. I accepted and within a week left the sanatorium and settled down in the children's home. On the same day, I began work.

*

Work, work . . . Once I started work, in November 1946, I did not stop for years, with only short breaks for giving birth to my children, for changing jobs, careers and countries, for learning new languages. Set aside the thirty-three years of my working life, the coaching job in the orphanage now seems only a brief episode. Yet it was crucial: I now moved from the world of adolescence to the world of commitments and responsibilities.

*

I was put in charge of a group of sixteen youngsters aged fifteen up. Sophie was one of them. Like everyone else she was supposed to call me 'Miss' – on the order of the director's wife. I was very young, she said, and some of my pupils were my own age; keeping a distance was of great importance.

It was terribly hard, though. The girls in my group longed to be friends; the boys tried to make passes at me. As a teacher, however, I quickly gained their respect. This was easy. Nearly all these children had spent most of their lives in exile, wandering across the Soviet Union, until they were finally sent to a home in Uzbekistan. Although they had on and off attended local schools they had not learnt much. When the home with its director and his wife was repatriated to Poland, the children found themselves lost in Polish schools: they knew very little about Polish history and literature, they had never learnt Latin or French, and they could hardly write in Polish. And here was I, competent and ready to help.

My work started in the afternoon when my pupils came home from school, and lasted till late at night. I catered for individual needs, teaching no more than three children and often only one at a time. Within an evening I had to switch from Polish to French, from Latin to History, and, more often than not, to my pet hate, Maths. I also helped two girls who needed to learn English because they hoped to be taken by a rich uncle to America. I did what I could to teach them the little I knew myself.

My duties were not confined to teaching. I was the overall mentor and tutor of the group, responsible for their cleanliness and clothing, as well as their good behaviour. The director's wife insisted that I teach them good manners and watch their language. They badly needed it. Having lived rough and without parental care for most of their childhood, they had become awkward and rude. During lessons and at table I tried hard to improve their manners but I could not help blushing when they swore. To make it worse, the boys greatly enjoyed my confusion and went on and on with their obscenities which often I could not even understand.

Having been forbidden to spend my free time with Sophie or with any of my charges, I was very lonely. The two other tutors, in charge of the younger groups, were much older and we had little in common. I shared a little room at the back of the house with one of them. She was a sullen, sour war widow who seldom spoke and saw me as an intruder, since my arrival had deprived her of her privacy. Once a week, on her day off, I would look after the youngest group for the morning. I liked this more than anything else. I enjoyed playing with the little children and they were very fond of me. They all longed for love and maternal care. There were two little sisters aged six and eight who did not even remember their parents. All they could remember was the Asian orphanage. They were beautiful, with huge black eyes and fine features; but they were both totally bald, having lost their hair from an earlier disease and malnutrition. These two bald girls would often call on me as I sat lonely and brooding in my room. Or little Leo would knock gently at my door – a little seven-year-old philosopher whose precocious wisdom alienated him from other children. These were the bright moments in my restricted life in the children's home.

Sophie had told me about Zionist undercurrents among my pupils, but this was kept such a secret that some time passed before I could become involved. The only grown-up who served as a link between the youngsters and the Zionist organisation outside the home was the storekeeper Roza. Since Sophie knew of my Zionist leanings, Roza eventually accepted me as her aide, though she belonged to Hashomer Hatzair, an organisation which was at loggerheads with the one I had belonged to. My part in the game was to serve as a link between Roza herself and Jakob, my eldest and most serious pupil, who was the leader of the Zionist cell in my group. I would meet Roza casually when collecting laundry from the store, hear news from her and later pass messages to Jakob as I helped him with his homework. It was much safer this way since any direct contact between the storekeeper and a pupil would have seemed strange to the director and have aroused his suspicions.

The director and his wife were an unpleasant couple. He belonged to the Polish Workers' Party and reminded us of it every time he opened his mouth. No day went by without one of his sloganeering speeches. His wife would chime in. The children hardly listened: most of them did not care for the Party's new order, or any social order for that matter. The only comfort the director could draw was one enthusiastic pupil, fifteen-year-old Dora. Dora was a bright, well-read girl. She looked down on all her fellow inmates as being less intelligent; she was despised in her turn by them for her mean nature and the privileges with which it was rewarded. She was the apple of the director's eye and was often invited to his and his wife's private rooms and table, which was said to be spread with delicacies unknown to the other children or to the members of staff. Dora was also the director's ear. With her in my group I never felt at ease. Once, trying in vain to explain the meaning of *accusativus cum infinitivo* to a very backward boy, I became so nervous that I couldn't help lighting a cigarette. Before I had time to finish it the director's wife burst into the classroom, sniffing around, indignant. She told me off in front of my pupils and threatened to sack me if I continued to smoke. There was no doubt as to who had summoned her just in time to catch me red-handed.

No one was safe with Dora around, not least those children who were preparing to leave for Palestine and secretly at night tried to learn some Hebrew or read the books I passed on to them from Roza. The manager hated the very idea of Zionism and always cited it in his speeches as being among the most rabid enemies of the new Poland. Had he discovered what was going on under his roof, he would certainly have stopped the youngsters from leaving the country and have administered an exemplary punishment; he would have also sacked the staff involved. Luckily, he suspected nothing, despite Dora being only too eager to inform. Instead, he boasted of giving shelter to the most loyal team of children, and educating the future champions of

Socialism. This misconception went unquestioned and gained him high praise from the authorities. He was said to run an exemplary home. Representatives of the educational establishment, of the Party, of children's homes from all over the country visited his institution time and again, to see how it worked, to take notes, to follow his example. Every time an official visit was announced, the children and staff were put on alert, the house was cleaned from basement to loft, inmates were issued with clean clothes. The menu was carefully chosen. When the visitors arrived Dora played hostess. She would show them round and explain that the home was run by the staff and children together; that the director never took any decisions without the approval of the Children's Committee; that we all lived in harmony like a big, close-knit family. Later, at table, sitting next to the most important guest, she would propose a toast to the success of the director, the beloved, the righteous, the most committed builder of the children's happy future.

News from the outside world only occasionally penetrated the secluded world of the children's home and even then was only brought in by the official Party paper or the director himself. In January 1947 the approaching elections for the first *Sejm** of the Polish People's Republic became the main item for discussion by children and staff. In fact, the issues involved were never discussed. Instead, the director would explain how important the forthcoming event was for the future of the country and for all of us. There was, he roared, a deadly struggle going on between the democratic parties and the people's enemies, who with the desperation of a dying beast were fighting for power. He appealed to us to face the enemy with clenched fists on the day of the election. Nobody knew what exactly he meant and nobody cared, except perhaps for Dora.

On the eve of 19 January the director told me to prepare myself and the children in my group for an early departure next morning. Surprised, I remarked that most of my pupils were not yet eighteen and thus not entitled to vote. But the director grinned at me sourly and said it was perfectly all right.

* Parliament

In the morning, a big lorry sent by the local authorities was tightly packed with all members of the staff and fourteen pupils from the eldest group. Two remaining youngsters, a very short girl and a retarded boy with the face of a nine-year-old, were told to stay at home. We were driven to Otwock, the nearest local town.

Many lorries were already parked in front of the polling station when we arrived. Crowds of farmers brought from the surrounding villages were guided to the building by the leaders of local party organisations who carried white-and-red or red-only banners. We had to queue for a long time before reaching the long row of tables on which the lists of voters were displayed. Behind the tables, in the middle of the large hall, stood a huge ballot-box. There was a single half-concealed booth in a far-off corner. I spelled out my name for the man at the table, trying to explain that since, as far as I knew, I had been registered in Warsaw, I could not possibly be on his list. But he said it was all right and ticked off an item on the list. Surprised, I peeped over his shoulder and saw it was a man's name: Stanislaw Nowak. I tried to draw his attention to the mistake, but the man quickly gave me an unsealed envelope with a ballot paper and turned to the next voter. Then someone pushed me towards the ballot-box with a firm instruction to drop the envelope straight into it. But I wanted to see the list of candidates before I dropped it in, so I stopped on my way and took it out of the envelope. The candidates of the democratic bloc were listed at the top, those of the reactionary Polish Peasant Party (PSL) underneath. I knew that if I left the list unmarked, this would mean a vote for the first names on the list. To vote for PSL, the opposition, I would have to go to the booth and delete the top names. I had little time to reflect, however, since my boss, with his arm round my shoulders, was pushing me to the ballot-box. Before I could open my mouth to say, 'I won't be a minute!' my envelope with the list of candidates intact slipped into the slit and disappeared.

The democratic bloc came out of the elections triumphant – the majority of the nation, over 80 per cent of voters, had supported the new regime. Deep in my heart I was not displeased. I hated anything which reminded me of the past: nationalism, the pre-war hapless politicians, the regime which had harboured and nurtured anti-Semitism. I would have voted against all this of my own free will if I had been free to. But I was not allowed to, I was forced to take part in a swindle and for this reason I also hated those who promoted the fraud: the Party. And my boss most of all.

I longed to leave the home. It was not easy, though, because of my lungs. I had to stay in the country for some time yet. Besides, I could hardly give up my free keep, my allowance of clothing and salary.

Some time towards the spring six of my pupils left for Palestine. The secret was kept to the last moment. The director learned of their departure only when he saw six empty chairs at the supper table. By this time the culprits were already on the train and approaching the frontier. It was too late to stop them. His rage was unbounded. An inquiry was launched, every child and member of staff was questioned. Not much was learnt, however. All the same, the director sacked Roza. Perhaps she answered him back when being questioned; or perhaps Dora sniffed out her role in the affair. Sophie and her friends who had been involved in the conspiracy but for the time being had stayed behind, were never found out or denounced. Neither was my part in the affair. Nobody suspected me of any mischief: such a good, quiet girl with such an innocent look in her somnolent eyes . . . So, I could stay and continue my work with the much reduced group, until I was ready to leave the children's home.

*

In our spare bedroom, used only to put up friends who come to see us from afar and stay for days or weeks, there is an enormous ancient chest of drawers where I keep the relics of our past: bundles of old letters tied up with coloured ribbons; big envelopes bulging with fading photographs; the milk teeth of my three daughters – impossible to tell which tooth belonged to which; Lena's thick plait cut off when she was six, on the day her sisters were born; stacks of my children's drawings that mainly show ourselves: five red or green monsters in front of square cottages with tall chimneys and still taller puffs of black smoke; my mother's keepsakes which I inherited when she died; greetings cards from friends all over the world; old theatre tickets, old concert programmes, old records of a happy life. There are piles of these things, the passing years adding still more and more. It would be even more had it not been for the Polish customs officers, who took it upon themselves to decide what memories their former fellow-citizen should be allowed to keep. Although I am a trained librarian, I store my keepsakes in a total mess, mementos of our early years mixed up with recent ones, snapshots of my babies next to their wedding photographs, Konrad's first love letters among those, equally loving, that he wrote after thirty-odd years of our married life.

I had intended to put all this in order when I retired, but years have passed since then and I still can't find time – or, maybe the inclination – to deal with it in earnest. I think it is too soon, my life is still too busy. Let's wait until real old age. So, only on and off do I open one of the drawers to put something in and then fish at random for a letter or two. Last time, when I was tucking in Christmas cards, I came across a letter from my mother's fondly guarded bundle. It was a letter I had written to her from the children's home.

Sosmowo, 12 February 1947

Dearest Mama,

Oh, how I miss you! I feel so lonely, so sad and there's no way I can come and have a good cry in your arms. No, don't be frightened: nothing has happened to me or Sophie, we are both perfectly well, though very seldom together. My work is all right, more or less; the kids tiring but not too bad, after all; sometimes I feel they really need me. So, not counting my dreadful boss, everything is fine and there's no need to worry – I'll survive again.

The only thing is, Mama, that I'm already twenty and still

have no plans or hope for the future. There was so little joy in my past, and I can't see any ahead: I'll wither if I stay in this country; I'll waste away if I leave.

Please, tell your friend that I can't possibly take up her suggestion. Sorry. Her nephew is certainly handsome, to judge by the enclosed photograph (his eyes are blue, his hair is blond, I presume!); and Australia must be a most attractive place; and what she says about his estate and wealth sounds awfully tempting. Yet, my dearest Mama, do I need to explain it to you? Are you not the one responsible for my romantic soul? I will never accept a marriage deal, never ever will I marry a man I don't love and who doesn't love me. So, I'll remain lonely for the rest of my life, since I have already been in love and loved, and this is over and can't possibly happen to me again. This is one more reason why I feel so sad and why I need you so much.

I left the children's home and returned to my mother in April 1947. There were more jobs than people at this time, so very soon I settled down as a typist in the Youth Department of the Central Committee of Polish Jews. I had never used a typewriter before but no one seemed to bother, I would learn to type while working. Nobody was shocked either when I handed in my first piece of typing densely spotted with corrections, the carbon copy printed in negative on the back of the top page.

Seven or eight people were employed in the Department. They were all my bosses. Their work was to settle young Jewish people who had survived the German occupation or were returning from Russia. They dealt with the housing, employment and education of the young people in their own particular way, since they all came from different political camps or groupings: Communists, socialists and Zionists of all shades. They argued loudly with each other all day long while I typed their contradictory letters and instructions, ever faster and better as time went by. I never took part in their quarrels and kept my views to myself. But with thoughts of my former boss still fresh in my mind, I strongly resented the two who belonged to the Polish Workers' Party.

The time then came when I could postpone no longer the question of what to do next. I applied to the Academy of Social and Political Sciences to study journalism, and, after an entry examination, was admitted for the autumn term. Meanwhile, in May 1947, I joined a Zionist organisation called Gordonia, or rather a students' club affiliated to this organisation.

Like the *kvutza* to which I had belonged a year earlier, the club aimed to prepare its members for life in Palestine. Its programme, however, was different. We were supposed to study hard in order to acquire proper professional skills before we left Poland to settle down individually in the cities of our new homeland. This kind of future seemed to suit me better than life in a rural commune. Gordonia's political standpoint suited me, too: it appeared to care for social equality no less than I did myself. So I joined the club enthusiastically and became its keenest member. For a while I truly belonged again; this time, luckily, not because of having TB.

Typing non-stop all morning and afternoon, spending most of my evenings in the club, doing all kinds of jobs for Gordonia sometimes till late at night – all this left little time for brooding. Besides, I was no longer lonely: I shared my club work with a boy. We spent long hours together. Soon we became a couple.

Lucjan was my age, tall and slim, not blond but not quite dark, neither plain nor particularly handsome. He had lost all his family during the war but seemed to manage easily on his own. His heart was set on leaving Poland; meanwhile he worked as a clerk and studied law. Our entanglement just happened. It was not a love affair. Love had nothing to do with it. It was, perhaps, something one does as an act of lost hope. I was waiting for the only thing that mattered: for the remote, the unknown, the dream-like homeland of the Jews.

· 3 ·

Slowly, haltingly, the plane is taking off. The rumble of giant engines muffles the soft Hebrew song playing in the cabin. There is a long pause, a moment of tense stillness, and then a sudden jerk. Now the machine gathers momentum; it speeds up along the runway and up into thick clouds. A flash of brightness, sharp as an electric knife, cuts across the cabin. Halfway between earth and sky, fastened in by the seat belt, pressed into my chair, for a short while I feel removed from the real world. Is this what one feels at the moment of death – this emptiness, this suspension between being and being no more? If so, there is no need to fear dying.

A quick glance down through the cabin window: the earth swings aslant with its patchy fields and winding roads. Somewhere there, far below, someone is starting to long for me. Here, above the clouds, in the midst of brightness, I already long for him. Why must we ever part?

The warning lights overhead go out, we can relax now. People unfasten their belts, light their cigarettes, make themselves comfortable. In Hebrew, then in English, the pilot tells us about our flight: soon we shall cross the Channel and fly over Germany and Switzerland, then over the Alps and the Greek Islands. Drinks and food are being served. The stewards trundle their trolleys down the aisle offering duty-free goods. The day quickly retreats and light drifts away. We are sailing through darkness now. Some passengers play cards, some others are dozing. Nobody seems to worry that we might be hijacked.

A piercing pressure in my ears – the descent has begun. The sparkling lights of Tel Aviv emerge from darkness far below. The Hebrew song comes on again: 'We brought you peace.' Peace? . . . But there is no time for bitter reflection. My eyes fill with inescapable tears. Because down there, in the sultry night, in the warm air that smells of orange blossom, my love, my daughter Lena, is waiting for me.

I can hardly remember how many times I have gone through all this since we moved to England and left Lena behind. Ten, perhaps twelve take-offs from the British chill; ten, perhaps twelve landings in the fragrant heat. Each time she is waiting for me, ever more adult and more beautiful. Her husband Daniel will be waiting there, too. We will drive in their little car through the pitch-dark night and talk nineteen to the dozen, trying to make up for all the time we have been apart. Then, suddenly, after a sharp bend, from behind a rock Jerusalem emerges ablaze with lights, perched upon hills over the dark valleys. This is where Lena lives.

*

She burst into tears when, in the spring of 1968, we told her we had decided to leave Poland. She was eighteen and in her first year at university. She wouldn't listen and locked herself for hours in her room. Towards evening she calmed down a little and began to talk. She said she loved Poland and couldn't imagine living anywhere else. She insisted that the same was true for us: we would never be happy elsewhere. We knew she was right. But there was no other way and we told her so. Too wise not to understand, she burst into tears again. Little by little and shyly, she confessed that it was not only love for her country that made her feel so rooted in Polish soil – there was also a boy.

When two months later, on midsummer night, we all stealthily and wordlessly squeezed into our overloaded car and set off on our long journey to the frontier, anxiously looking back lest we be followed, Lena cried her heart out: she was leaving her boy, her first love. He had been jailed during the student riots and kept there without trial since March. She could not say goodbye to him, she did not know whether he felt for her as she did for him – they had never dared to speak about their feelings. They might never see each other again.

So she cried as we crossed the frontier, and cried when we made our way through Czechoslovakia, which at that time was enjoying its short-lived freedom. In the refugee camp near Vienna where we stopped for three weeks she heard from newcomers that soon after our departure Daniel had been released. For a while she beamed with joy. But soon we saw her sad again: how could she tell whether he wanted to leave Poland and if so where he planned to go? So, while her twelve-year-old sisters sparkled with excitement and revelled in the greatest adventure of their short lives, she could find no consolation – neither in the busy streets of Vienna, the first Western city she had explored, nor in the beauty of Venice. Her mind was still far away when, after four days of sailing, our ship reached Israel at the port of Haifa.

She took to work with frantic determination. Starting, as we all did, with scribbling from right to left the unfamiliar Hebrew characters, she progressed at an amazing speed. Ambitious like her father, like him always so keen to learn and to achieve perfection in whatever she did, desperate not to let time slip by, she was ready in only a couple of months to resume her university studies. Then we had to leave her on her own in Jerusalem as Konrad had been offered a senior university post in Tel Aviv.

Living on her own in a stifling hotel room in an Arab quarter, Lena worked extremely hard. She had no interest in fun or boys, not even her own appearance. The only thing she thought of, apart from her studies, was the boy she had left behind. She heard from Daniel once or twice, but his letters were too vague to know how he felt for her and what he intended to do.

Seven hard months went by filled with the effort of finding our feet in this exotic world. One January day Lena received a message: in a few hours Daniel and his family would be landing at Tel Aviv airport. Abandoning her lectures, she set off at once from Jerusalem which on that unusual day was covered with snow. Our hearts full of strong feelings for this courageous young man whom we had met only once before he was arrested, Konrad and I drove to the airport, too.

It was late and dark; the last-remaining scraps of fast-melting snow glittered in the headlights on the palm trees. But the airport hall buzzed with an impatient crowd. The black figures of orthodox Jews with their long beards and winding side-curls mingled with the green uniforms of soldiers, suntanned kibbutz-nikim, old people still bearing their mid-European style with pride. They were all waiting for their loved ones.

In the midst of this throng we found Lena. Her clothes in disarray, her hair blown by the wind, she could hardly hide her anxiety: perhaps she was here in vain? She wasn't the only one waiting nervously for Daniel – there were other friends who had come to meet him – that brave student who had been jailed and subjected to endless cross-questioning. His relatives waited for him too.

When, after a long delay, Daniel and his parents at last appeared in the hall, there was no opportunity for Lena to talk to him in private. The family was immediately surrounded by relatives and friends, smothered with embraces and showered with questions. Excited and confused, Daniel walked along as if in a dream and seemed not to notice Lena who shyly drew back. And when they finally came face to face, he only stopped for a moment to ask for her new address. Distressed and resentful, she gave him ours. Then he vanished from sight into a car and was driven away. It was a heart-breaking night for Lena, so we took her home and let her cry.

Next day, early in the morning, Daniel turned up at our suburban flat. Kind-hearted, homely, his brown short-sighted eyes warmly smiling from behind thick lenses, he became a member of our family in a most simple way. There was no doubt as to why he had come to Israel. He soon left with Lena for Jerusalem, to learn Hebrew and resume his studies.

Two years passed before they got married. Reluctant to marry in accordance with the strict religious rules of Jewish weddings, they had to wait for a chance to travel abroad. One summer they took a short trip to Sweden and were married there at the Stockholm Town Hall.

It has been many years now since the morning that Daniel came to find Lena. They both studied then worked hard. Two children were born, grew up and went to school. They all live in a beautiful house built of bright Jerusalem stone, surrounded by other bright houses and by trees that in spring light up with golden blossom. From the windows of their modern flat they can see Jerusalem settled on the rocks, basking in the sun with her churches, her mosques, her flocks grazing in the valleys. At night, the wailing muezzin calls out with his plaintive prayer from a nearby minaret. But they never hear it. Tired out, they sleep soundly before a new day of their hard, successful life begins.

At first they thought of going somewhere else, of trying other ways. The world seemed so huge and so unexplored. But little by little they have learned to feel at home here, to love what is beautiful and fight what is wrong.

Our story was different. We could not stay for ever. We were no longer young, our past was too full, our experience too bitter. It was too late to struggle again and we had no will to conform. So, after three years of a comfortable life, we decided to start from scratch again and settle in England. This time only the twins came with us.

*

My short yearly visit has come to an end. The plane takes off from the parched soil. My heart sinks at the thought of parting again. We fly over the sea and over the Alps, and plunge deep again into the clouds that shroud the British Isles. The overhead lights go on, the descent is well under way. Sweet expectation warms my tired heart: because down there, in the chilly mist, his hair a little more grey than last year, someone is waiting for me.

· 4 ·

I had to wait for him for more than twenty years. The closer the day came the less hope I had I would ever find him.

The beginning of my student life in the autumn of 1947 was a time of stress and disappointment. I would rush to the Academy after work. All lectures and seminars started late in the afternoon because most students had to work during the day to earn their living. Thousands of people attended the three faculties, most of them trying to make up for the wasted years of war. Many were still in the army and wore military uniforms. The vast lecture theatres and spacious seminar rooms were always full. I would burst in at the very last moment and leave immediately the lecture was over, always hurrying, with no time or wish to talk to anybody. At night, in the little room I shared with Mother, I would stay up late, bent over books and papers. It was the first time I had ever studied social problems, economics, law or social history. It was also my first serious encounter with Marx and Engels, whose works I had now to study in depth. I plunged into this reading with ever-growing interest. The ideas struck me as sound and fair. I tried to resist their spell by calling to mind the people I knew who had preached and practised Marxism in its most crude and repellent form: my old-time boss or those who had rigged the election. The more I read, however, the stronger I felt that the ideas were right and that the social order proposed by Marxists was fair. But I knew it was beyond human grasp because of the inadequacy of the people who were setting out to produce it.

Working and studying six days a week, I had very little time left for Gordonia. I would drop into the club on Sundays, but only to see people and hear news. Then, feeling guilty at wasting time, I would hurry back home to dive into my pile of books which never seemed to get smaller.

My liaison with Lucjan was on the wane. The more I became involved in my studies, the less I cared for him. Our meetings were less and less frequent; they became shorter and were always tense. I would criticise Lucjan for neglecting his studies and for his shifty ways of getting on in the world. He insisted on our getting married and grew impatient with my repeated refusals. More often than not, he would leave in anger, slamming the door behind him. Many a time we decided to split up, but a couple of days later he would come round again. It was hard to turn him away and give him up entirely. I was afraid of loneliness more than anything else. So we dragged on this way throughout the first term. Only at Christmas, after a serious quarrel, did I feel I could not carry on with Lucjan any longer. This time I must have sounded firm: he did not turn up again, neither during the holidays nor at the start of the second term.

Downcast, I attended my classes with the diligence of an exemplary schoolgirl, missing only a few when I had to stand in for one of my bosses and stay longer at work. So many people from the three faculties crowded into the lecture theatres that it was impossible to get to know all my fellow students even by sight. There were always new faces, and even more when a host of latecomers joined the course at the start of the second term. The lectures and seminars for the journalism students had far smaller numbers, but even here the crowd was too large and too anonymous for a shy girl like myself to make friends. Some students did get to know each other and formed groups, but I always stayed apart and alone.

One woman student among the 'journalists' I had always found interesting. She was a few years older than myself, good-looking and well-dressed. She also seemed somehow brighter than the rest. Her name was Krystyna. Though not at all shy, she hardly ever spoke to anyone, keeping herself at a distance like myself. I longed to be friends with her, but she paid me no attention and I never dared make the first step.

One day at the beginning of February I went to a seminar on literary criticism. The tutor was a well-known writer and his seminars always drew large audiences. About a hundred student journalists gathered in the seminar hall that afternoon. As usual, I took a seat in one of the back rows and was looking forward to an hour of intellectual delight. The tutor, a heavy middle-aged man, was already spreading his notes on his desk when Krystyna appeared in the door. This time she was not alone: a tall handsome officer bearing the rank of Polish Army captain followed closely behind her. As they hurriedly made their way down the aisle, his eyes for a split second met mine. It was a shock: never before had I seen eyes like those – a pair of brilliant, ripe plums brimming with the joy of life.

The handsome couple passed quickly by and found themselves two seats in one of the front rows. The seminar began. The tutor bustled about his desk, rustled his sheets and gave a fascinating talk about a remarkable new novel. He then called upon the audience to discuss the book. I sat numb, completely unable to follow, my startled mind carried away by Krystyna's man. With a pang of envy I thought how lucky she was to own him. Yes, I imagined she owned him. He belonged to her and even to stare at him was like trespassing. Nevertheless, I could not help glancing at the back of his dark head. Then, suddenly, something happened that made my heart stop: the officer turned round, his plum-like eyes fixed on me. It lasted only a second – and then all I could see of him again was his black, slightly wavy hair.

Soon I saw him raise his hand. He stood up and stepped forward to the rostrum. Facing the audience, he began to speak. I listened fascinated. His account of the novel was thoughtful, original and striking, sparkling with witty remarks. The students listened engrossed now and then bursting into laughter. Obviously pleased, the tutor nodded his approval.

Then the seminar came to an end and I saw Krystyna leave with her captain. They walked away arm in arm. They formed a splendid couple. I dragged home, more lonely than ever. That night I told Mother about a Prince Charming who would never be mine.

Some time passed before I saw him again. He seemed to miss lectures quite often, perhaps too busy to go to them all. This time I met him on a Sunday. I was queuing outside a cinema with my old friend Teresa. He was in the same queue with another officer. As we all entered the foyer, he suddenly spoke to me. It was not a 'hello' or a 'good evening' or anything as polite as that. He curtly asked why I had missed a shorthand class which was a compulsory part of our syllabus. He sounded bossy and rude. Taken aback I hardly answered and dismissed him with a reluctant grin.

The film I had come to see was a French comedy – *Three Gentlemen Called Luis*. That is all I remember – I didn't watch the film, my thoughts were too far away. I wondered where Krystyna was and could not help feeling pleased that she wasn't with him.

More was to come. Over the following fortnight I watched the couple split up. They came to lectures separately and sat miles apart. Now I could with impunity send the lonely captain some of my best languishing glances. This I did quite often – though I still thought him a rough army bumpkin. He, for his part, brazenly answered my glances, not even trying to be discreet. I melted under his burning gaze and forgot his faults.

Near the end of the second term, on Wednesday 17 March, I was taken ill and did not go to work. I had a sore throat and temperature and stayed in bed all morning. But in the afternoon I got up – there was a lecture on criminal law that evening that I could not bear to miss.

The weather was awful, the worst of March gales. I arrived earlier than usual and found the lecture theatre still half empty. I suddenly thought, why don't I change my normal habit and sit at the front? So I chose a seat in the middle of an empty front row.

I did not have to wait long before the captain arrived. He swept the huge theatre with his sharp gaze and spotted me at once. And there he was, smart and radiant, walking straight towards me. With a broad smile that seemed to bring golden sparks to his eyes, he bowed, asking my permission to sit next to me. Taken aback by this unseemly gallantry, I gave him a coy nod. Encouraged, he whispered his name and kissed my hand right in front of all the students now surging into the hall. This was incredible. It was beyond my understanding. His behaviour denied the fashionable style of 'democratic' manners and it shattered my image of him as a military boor.

During the lecture we sat very close taking hasty notes, not looking at each other. My mind was full of the intricacies of penal law, but at the same time somewhere deep in my breast there rose an intimation of great happiness to come.

When the lecture was over I made no haste to leave. I deliberately took my time in tidying up my notes and putting them into my bag: I wanted the captain to make his own choice, to say goodbye and go if he wished to. But he did not. He waited for me and we left together, pushing our way through the noisy crowd. Out of the corner of my eye I could see Krystyna leaving on her own. I wasn't sorry for her; she wasn't the kind of a person you'd easily feel pity for.

Outside in the street, I stopped to say goodbye to the captain – I expected him to turn right, like all officers who lived in the southern part of town. My tram-stop was off to the left and I told him so. But he said this was a lucky coincidence and turned left with me.

We walked along in freezing rain, lashed by the wind. We jumped over deep puddles landing in a slushy mixture of water and snow. The street was poorly lit so we could hardly see each other. The wailing of the wind made conversation impossible. I also had a terrible pain in my inflamed throat whenever I tried to speak. But it was the happiest walk of my life.

In an empty draughty square my empty draughty tram was already waiting. I assumed the captain would be taking another one, so I stopped again to say goodbye. But he said this was a lucky coincidence and followed me onto the tram.

Only then did we begin to talk. He said I looked like his sister – I thought this was a rather hackneyed way of starting conversation with a girl. I had expected something better from him. Then, to my great surprise, he drew from his breast-pocket a snapshot of a young woman who truly resembled me. Another surprise came when he told me that his sister Tova lived in a kibbutz in Palestine. I would have loved to have heard all about her life and what he himself thought of the Zionist movement. But the captain was obviously reluctant to elaborate and quickly switched to a different subject. He was an enthusiastic theatre-goer, he said, and wanted to know whether I had seen the new musical *The Straw Hat* which was being played at one of the few theatres that had been rebuilt in the city and had had excellent reviews. I had been dying to see this musical, but couldn't afford the ticket. Of course, I did not mention this – I just said I hoped to see *The Straw Hat* in the future. 'What a lucky coincidence,' exclaimed the captain. He was going to see it on Sunday, and had, by chance, a spare ticket. Would I be kind enough to accept his invitation?

My heart jumped with joy and for a moment I was frightened lest he might have noticed; I always dreaded being taken for an easy girl. So, biting back my dearest wish, I said I would have to think it over and could only give him an answer at the shorthand lesson on Friday. The tram was just pulling up at my stop, so I got up ready to say goodbye. But he got up too and followed me. We left the tram together. This time he forgot to mention the lucky coincidence. He saw me to the gate of my house and only then did we part.

Shivering with fever, and in great pain, I tried desperately to convey to Mother what had happened in the last few hours. She was excited but alarmed, and called in a doctor. Indeed, I was seriously ill. Tossing feverishly all night, I dreamed a restless dream about the captain. His handsome face smiled at me from under his military cap or ran away from me and vanished in the darkness.

In the morning I woke sober but terrified. Supposing I were to lose him? There was no way I could meet him on Friday; no way I could go to the theatre with him on Sunday. The Easter break was due to start the following week, so I would not see him for at least five weeks. Nor would I be able to explain what had happened. He would certainly take it as an insult and would give me up altogether. Something had to be done at once. I asked Mother for help.

It was hard to find someone in postwar Warsaw if you did not know much about them. There were only a few telephones, so the directory was of little help. To make it worse, I knew only the captain's surname. His first name, his address, even his age were unknown to me. With little hope but with every desire to help, Mother promised to try her best and left for work. I knew I could rely on her. Her life as a widow was drab and sorrowful, and she flatly rejected any chance of remarrying – she therefore invested all her hopes and fears in her two daughters. She would have brought down the heavens to make us happy. In the evening she returned triumphant: she had hunted everywhere for the captain's address and had finally succeeded.

I sat up in bed and wrote him the shortest letter ever:

19th March 1948

Dear Captain,
Please don't feel offended: I cannot accept your kind invitation to the theatre on Sunday because I have been taken ill and have to stay in bed for quite a long time.
Wishing you good holidays,
J.L. (your colleague at the Academy)

It was Thursday night and it seemed unlikely that the letter would reach the captain by post before Monday. Mother came to my rescue again. She offered to deliver the message herself. And so she did on Friday morning, leaving it with the janitor of the house where the captain lived.

Now I could peacefully abandon myself to my illness, no longer fearing that the captain might take offence. All the same, I felt sick at heart at the thought of not seeing him for all those endless weeks.

On Sunday morning, however, my longing, as well as my peace of mind, came to an abrupt end. There was a gentle knocking at the front door and Mother went to answer, wondering whoever it could be at such an unusual time. From my bed I could hear her exclaim 'Ah!' and then 'Oh!' in the corridor. Then she returned flushed and announced in a frantic whisper that *he* was here asking to see me. In fact, the captain's head had already appeared high above her shoulder as he tried to edge his way into the room. He was dressed in civilian clothes with an elegant hat, and looked younger than usual. I wondered how Mother had guessed it was *him*. But she seemed to be in no doubt at all about it and with her charming, warm smile she invited him to sit down next to my bed on the only chair we possessed. The captain smiled back no less warmly but declined to take a seat, saying he had only dropped by for a second to ask how I was, and did not want to bother us any longer. Besides, he added, his friend was waiting for him downstairs. He did not seem to be at all embarrassed but his slim fingers played nervously with a tin cigarette case. As for myself, I was overwhelmed with joy and very anxious not to show it. I felt terribly uneasy at our shabby room stuffed with its shabby belongings, and even more so at my faded, plain nightdress and the washed-out bed-sheets. But I desperately wanted him to stay. I said he could smoke if he wished to. Eagerly he sat down and lit one of his strong cigarettes. We talked for a short while about something as tame as the weather or flu. Then a sharp whistle came from the courtyard: the friend had tired of waiting. The captain got up. 'Now I know your letter was true,' he said, looking straight into my eyes. He kissed Mother's hand, then mine, and left in a hurry. He had forgotten his cigarette case and it stayed on my bedside table.

When on Monday evening he returned to reclaim his property, I was alone at home. Mother had gone to see Uncle Jerzy and was not expected back till late at night. I was still very ill and could hardly get up, so I stayed in bed during his long visit. He sat by my bed in the twilight and we talked softly, no longer trying to hide how we felt about each other. He asked me whether I was free and I told him all about Lucjan. Then he told me about his affair with Krystyna and that it had been coming to an end long before he met me. So we were both free to love each other.

The following evening we spoke about our childhoods. He had been born and brought up in Poznan in a family of slender means.

He had experienced much hardship and had suffered from anti-Semitism. At the start of the war he and his parents had fled to the Soviet Union where they had lived starving for many years. Nonetheless, at sixteen he had managed to graduate from a high school there and had for a couple of years attended a Russian University. Later, at eighteen, he joined the Polish Army in Russia and became a junior officer. He was sent to the front. He served in an artillery unit all the way to the Baltic sea, was then wounded but recovered just in time to take part in the final battle of Berlin. He was awarded several medals, gradually rose to the rank of captain and now served as a political officer in a large unit stationed in Warsaw. His parents had returned safely from the Soviet Union and they all lived together in a small flat that had been given him by his unit for as long as he served. Konrad's eyes beamed with pride as he said he was a Communist and a member of the Polish Workers' Party. It was no surprise to me, I had suspected it from the beginning.

I was equally open with him. I told him I had been born into a wealthy family and brought up by a host of nannies and governesses. I had enjoyed luxuries that many a child had never dreamt of. He listened, a little upset, but brightened up when I said that this fortune had vanished with the war and that Mother and I now lived almost in squalor, as he could see for himself; we had to work hard and let Sophie stay in the children's home to make ends meet. Then I confessed I was a Zionist and an active member of Gordonia, ready to leave Poland and start a new life in Palestine. This was a blow to him. He turned pale, fell silent and left soon after, very upset. I thought I had lost him for ever.

He came back on Wednesday to say that I was for him more important than anything else in the world and I told him the same.

On Thursday we decided to marry.

On Friday he told Mother he wanted me as his wife and asked her for her permission. They were standing in the little corridor and Mother collapsed onto a heap of coals stored there.

On Saturday his friend Adam was finally brought in to admire the most beautiful girl in the world. A short, square officer in his

· 45 ·

thirties, he gave me a sharp look and shrugged his broad shoulders. 'All right,' he said, 'I didn't expect to find an Aphrodite here, anyway.' I hated him.

On Sunday Uncle Jerzy came to meet his future nephew and the date of our wedding was discussed. No decision was reached, however – I was still too poorly to get up.

Although we were very impatient we had to wait five months before we could get married. Konrad applied to his military authorities for permission to marry me. In reply he was ordered to submit several documents proving that I was a suitable person to be an officer's wife. They wanted to know all about my social background and political beliefs. I had to prove my health was sound, namely that I had never suffered from a venereal disease. They needed a certificate from the local council stating in black and white that I was 'morally flawless' – not a thief or a prostitute.

My recovery was very slow, so it was not until mid-April that I could start collecting the documents. The health certificate was easily obtained. No one was interested in my TB, so Uncle Jerzy, a doctor, needed no tests to confirm that I was healthy, not a VD carrier. Another relative of mine, Uncle Leo, an old Communist highly respected by the establishment for his past work, provided me with certificates from two high-ranking officials who happened to be close friends of his. They both declared that, despite my wealthy origins, I was a loyal citizen of the Polish People's Republic and fully trustworthy. My political involvements were fortunately overlooked in both statements: it did not occur to Uncle Leo that I had any political views whatsoever.

The last certificate, that of moral respectability, was the hardest to obtain. The local council had to make inquiries and though I was innocent I feared my landlord might speak against me. He had made overtures to both Mother and I when his wife was out. We had both repeatedly rejected him and he hated us. His wife knew about this and hated us too. If the local council had asked their opinion they might, I feared, say I was a thief and a whore. Fortunately, the Larks were not in favour with the council and were not asked for a reference at all. So, finally in July, I received my certificate of morality.

I never returned to work after my illness. I had had enough of the dreary typing that led nowhere. Konrad begged me not to look for another job. He argued that I should take more care of my health, concentrate on my studies and learn how to run a house. I knew he was right but would never admit it. The idea of being a housewife and living on my husband's income, for however short a time, seemed outrageous to me. These were our first arguments. Little by little, however, we came to an agreement: I promised not to go back to work till the following autumn and meantime to learn to cook.

My teacher and mentor in the matter of domestic science was Konrad's mother. She and I had had fond feelings for each other long before we met. Knowing me only from a photograph and from what Konrad had told her about me, she was very concerned about my health and frequently sent me jars of nourishing food and friendly letters. I felt terribly uneasy about taking food from someone I did not even know until I realised that I had been accepted in advance as a member of the family. I still had to prove I deserved this acceptance.

The crucial moment came when Mother and I, dressed in our Sunday best and with a huge bunch of yellow tulips, arrived at Konrad's family home for tea. We were both very nervous, like schoolgirls before an exam. The exuberant person who greeted us at the door filled my heart with rapture and awe from first sight. She was in her early fifties and very stout, wearing a full black dress adorned with a heavy amber necklace. Her long amber ear-rings framed a pale face of striking beauty. Her hair was slightly grey, her skin was fair and smooth, and her wise bottle-green eyes stared at me searchingly. The way she moved and spoke contained a youthful vigour. Shy and silent, I let her take my hand and lead me like a child into the room where my 'father' was waiting for me. The bald, toothless, ugly old man grinned awkwardly at me, mumbled a few faint words and won my heart at once: he was even more shy than myself.

The flat consisted of two little rooms, a kitchen and a bathroom. It was full of sunshine, perfectly tidy and clean, decorated with potted plants and replicas of great Russian paintings of the nineteenth century. It was such a sharp contrast to our own squalid room that I felt as though I had entered a world of luxury to which I didn't belong. To make things worse, I glanced in a big mirror hanging on the wall and, to my dismay, saw an unruly crop of dark hair heaped over a pair of terrified green eyes which seemed too big in the deathly pale face. My thick green woollen dress, intended to match my eyes, only stressed my sickly pallor and looked totally unsuitable for the warm spring day. I was sure Zofia must have noticed all this at a single glance.

We sat at a round table spread with an embroidered tablecloth eating delicious home-made cake and sipping strong tea. The conversation was hesitant, sustained mainly by the two mothers who seemed keen to find out about each other's lives. I shared my silence with the old man in unspoken mutual understanding. Konrad was unusually quiet, his eyes fixed on me, his face bright with pride and happiness. 'Look at her,' he seemed to be saying, 'Look what a beauty, what a treasure I've brought you.' And under his burning gaze all my worries and shyness disappeared. I felt beautiful and valuable again, and very much in love.

Zofia was far too wise to keep us long at table. As soon as the glasses were emptied and most of the cake eaten, she suggested a 'generation split' and ordered 'the young' to 'march off'. We did so with undisguised zeal and settled in the adjoining bedroom, leaving the door ajar. Konrad switched on the gramophone moved in for the occasion and played tunes from the film *Sun Valley Serenade*, very popular in Warsaw after the war. We danced a little and kissed a lot, with an awkward feeling that our three parents knew only too well what was going on behind the half-open door and fully approved.

Historic events were taking place in the Middle East that spring. On 14 May the State of Israel was proclaimed and recognised. The following day, war began between the Arabs and Jews. So far Konrad and I had tried to avoid a confrontation on the issue of Palestine, but now it could not be put off any longer. It soon became clear that Konrad not only had never considered living in

Palestine – he actually strongly disapproved of my involvement. Zionism, he claimed, like any other nationalism, was incompatible with his strong Communist beliefs. We all knew only too well what horrors nationalism could lead to and there was no reason to believe either that the Jews were the chosen nation or that their nationalism was any more justified or less dangerous than that of other peoples. There were Arabs living in Palestine, after all. Besides, he argued, the Jews are not a nation. They live all over the world, speak a thousand languages, are an organic part of the countries where they were born and brought up.

Outraged, I tried to make him see the anti-Semitism that Jews had suffered from wherever they had lived and which would continue as long as they lived dispersed; I had experienced this for long years and so had he in his childhood. Was it not reason enough for the Jews to struggle for their own state?

Unflinching in his faith, yet sound and clear in his reasoning, Konrad explained that there would be no room for anti-Semitism, or any other racial hatred, under Communism – this fairest of social systems, which would guarantee full equality between human beings regardless of language, race or creed. We were particularly lucky, he stressed, to have been born at the right time and in the right place to become active fighters for this noblest cause. The greatest of historical changes was happening before our eyes, here and now. To stand by as idle witnesses would be to miss a unique opportunity. Running away would be betrayal.

I listened enthralled. Here was the voice of an honest Communist; his arguments seemed sound and he truly believed in what he was saying. The idea of equality had always appealed to me. I had recently acquired a basic knowledge of Marxist theory and found it deeply convincing. But I had never so far met a Marxist I could trust. Here was the first – passionate and honourable – and my beloved. As he spoke, I searched feverishly for arguments to defend my Zionist views. But it was not easy: all I could do was to plead for a Marxist Jewish state. I argued that the fight for social justice could be fought everywhere in the world, provided we had our own fortress from which to fight. First we had to build this fortress – a home for the homeless Jews.

Konrad dismissed my ideas. He said I had lived in Poland for over twenty years, had been fed with Polish bread and culture, had survived the holocaust here – didn't I owe something to this country?

I fell silent, at a loss for further arguments. The only thing I knew for certain was that he would never go to Israel, and so neither would I. Strangely enough, I felt slightly relieved.

Shortly after the family tea party, Zofia paid me a surprise visit. It was on a weekday morning and I was at home alone. I heard her pant and puff noisily as she climbed the last few steps to our sixth-floor flat. She burst into my room gasping for breath, pretending not to look around. She dropped heavily onto my bed and sat there – the chair was too spindly for her heavy body. On the table she placed a big bag of home-made biscuits – a present for Mother and myself. I waited patiently for a long while until she got her breath back in order to speak. She had come to talk to me, she said, about things her son should never be told. She trusted I would keep them to myself. I promised to do so. All agog, I listened to the sad story of her family.

As long as she could remember, Zofia began, her husband had dreamed of emigrating to Palestine. In the late 1930s they had seriously considered settling there. Her daughter Tova wanted to go. Konrad was too young to be asked; Zofia, though hesitant, had never objected. They were about to leave when war broke out. Only Tova, by then nineteen, had managed to escape before it was too late.

As I already knew, Zofia continued, Father and Konrad and herself had escaped the approaching Germans and had spent the war in the Soviet Union. Life there was very hard – Zofia had worked as a cook in the workers' canteen. But the people had been very kind and understanding. Soon she became one of them, sharing their desperate fight for victory, their privations, their struggle for survival. And so it happened that both she and her young son got acquainted with Communism and fell under its spell. As soon as she returned from Russia she applied for membership of the Polish Workers' Party and was accepted at once. She was passionate and eager and profoundly grateful to the new regime for their flat, for her husband's steady job, for the promise of a bright future. Now at last they could live in peace and in comfort – had it not been for her husband's continued restlessness. Neither the war, nor Communism, nor the security of his present life, had ever put a stop to his dreams of leaving for Palestine. He never complained, even to his own son, but Zofia knew how he suffered as he lay in bed night after night sighing in despair. They both longed for Tova and there was no hope of her returning: she seemed very happy where she was, with her husband, children and her kibbutz.

Zofia fell silent and looked at me intently, trying to see whether I had guessed where this story was leading to. I had no idea. She resumed her tale, this time coming straight to the point.

Neither she nor her husband had ever thought of leaving for Palestine without their son, she said. It was because of him that they had returned to Poland instead of going straight there. When they had heard about my Zionist convictions, a sudden ray of hope had warmed their tired hearts: I was the only person in the world who might be able to change Konrad's views. They knew how much he loved me. He might agree to what I wanted if I tried very hard. And if he did, his father's life-long dream would at last come true; and the family would be together again.

I stared at Zofia in disbelief: was she trying to say that she would abandon her beliefs, surrender her Party card and emigrate? Yes, she said, she would. And her love for me would be infinite if I would help her. Bewildered, I promised her nothing. I knew I would never be able to change Konrad's faith, nor would I be willing to try.

June came, hot and dry. It was the end of the academic year, and we were working hard for exams – fourteen in the next five weeks. With so many students at the Academy, examinations were the only way that progress could be assessed. Shut up at home, buried in our papers, Konrad and I stopped seeing each other for a while. It was the time when I went to the Gordonia club to say goodbye: this short chapter of my life had come to an end.

This two-week break was a trying experience. We had no telephone so could not even talk to each other. Sometimes I wondered whether the past three months had really happened and whether Konrad would still love me when we met again. Surprisingly enough, Adam, the man I used to hate, suddenly proved a good friend: he called on us both daily bringing news.

Only when the exams had begun did we start meeting again, sitting next to each other or queuing for the orals. We often met Krystyna, and I finally got to know her. But the brief moments we spent with her in the corridor talking about the exams were very tense and hard for all three of us. We also met other students and made new friends. Many people took us for brother and sister. They said we looked extraordinarily similar. We began to feel quite incestuous and ran to hide ourselves after exams from their inquisitive glances.

By the middle of July the exams were over and we heaved a sigh of relief: we had both passed all fourteen of them – Konrad with the highest marks, I with a mixture of 'goods' and 'very goods'. Now it was time to think about our wedding. My 'moral purity' document had finally arrived and Konrad could at last submit a complete dossier of papers to his colonel. This colonel had become a very important figure in my life, though I had only met him a few times. Well into his forties, stiff and straight in his perfectly fitting uniform, with the balding head and piercing eyes of an intellectual, he commanded Konrad's total respect and admiration. As a pre-war Communist, he seemed to embody the highest ideals; his voice and judgement were those of the Party. Any word of disapproval from him would have been devastating to Konrad. I was in complete awe of him, and couldn't face him without feeling stupid and of no importance to the Cause. Waiting for his decision we both became a bundle of nerves. His answer came after a week: Konrad could marry me.

The date of the wedding was fixed for 18 August, the day of my twenty-second birthday. With no work, no studies and not even Gordonia Club, I had a full month of freedom ahead. I kept my promise to learn housewifery and spent most of my days with Zofia, while Konrad and his father were at work. She introduced me to the obscure world of cookery and housekeeping and taught me all sorts of useful things that I have never forgotten. We got on very well. I told her all about my family and listened to her tales of Konrad when he was a child. The main subject of Zofia's endless concern, however, was Tova. There had been no news from her since the war in the new State of Israel had begun. Day after day I ran downstairs to see whether any mail from her had arrived. I tried my best to comfort her despairing mother and to make her think of other things, but conversation always came back to Israel. However, Zofia never mentioned again her desire to emigrate – we had silently agreed not to discuss the matter.

Preparations for the wedding were largely taken out of my hands. Zofia took on the most demanding task – the wedding party. The matter of my moving house was extremely simple; the only thing I would be taking with me from home was an antique chest-of-drawers that had once belonged to my grandparents and had survived the war in the gardener's hut. This was easily packed with my few belongings and carried on a rickshaw to my new home. With money I had borrowed from Uncle Jerzy – he never accepted it back – I bought a piece of light-blue cloth and, for the first time in my life, made an appointment with a dressmaker. Since everybody insisted that my hair should be set for the occasion, I also made my first appointment with a hairdresser – a whole month in advance. And that was that: there was nothing left for me to do.

The day of the wedding arrived, hot and stifling from early dawn. The ceremony had been booked for 2 o'clock in the afternoon and the bridegroom with his best man were expected to arrive at our house an hour before to take me with Mother and Sophie to the registry office. Sophie had left the children's home on the previous day. Since I was leaving home, she could now move in and live with Mother. They were both getting ready for the solemn event and working hard to prepare all I needed too. So, all was carefully planned in advance and I had no need to worry. I put on a shabby summer dress from the war and went to the hairdresser's.

This proved to be a major operation. Noon was striking as I

reappeared in the street, changed beyond recognition. My long hair, which I usually wore loose, was now pinned up into a high dome shining with Brylcream. Two fresh rosebuds were fastened to this stiff construction and two curly strands of hair descended from it straight across my forehead, partly obstructing my view. My fingernails and toenails were varnished pink, the latter shamelessly protruding from my worn sandals. I hurried home and quickly sneaked into the staircase, anxious not to be seen by the neighbours in this strange attire. Gasping for breath, I stopped only to glance at my watch: luckily, I still had fifty minutes to make something of my appearance. But alas, when I opened the door, I was stunned by a frightening spectacle. In the middle of the narrow room, long before the appointed time, stood my beloved dressed in his gala uniform and medals, solemn and radiant like a rising moon. Lolling on the only chair, Adam proudly presented his heroic chest, which also shone with medals. The beds, the table, even the window sill were covered with festive dresses and silky underwear. Bewildered, Mother and Sophie, still in their dressing gowns, tried to look delighted. To make matters worse, Mr Lark, lured by the sounds of an unusual commotion, walked through the room up and down to see what was going on, while his wife, locked in the bathroom, was taking one of her endless baths, thus frustrating my only chance of retreat.

Incredible though it may sound, I still managed to get dressed in these circumstances. In my great haste I ruined my hair-do but this only made me feel better. To my surprise, I did not even hate Konrad for coming an hour too early, and still wanted to marry him. I only learned on my wedding day that from now on and for ever I would have to live in a hurry.

The wedding took place in the big building of the Bank of National Economy which had escaped wartime destruction and housed many important offices, including the registry. We drove there in three open military cars allocated for the occasion by the Colonel. He had sent his congratulations but declined to attend the ceremony. Apart from a handful of relatives, the only others present were our witnesses: Adam and my old friend Teresa. We all gathered in a big office that looked like any other big office except for a potted palm evidently placed there to mark the difference. The registrar looked like an ordinary clerk, though he wore a chain over his plain suit. There was no 'Here comes the bride' or anything like that, tape recorders had not yet arrived in Poland. Nonetheless, we felt very happy and moved, and not our usual selves. So, when asked whether I wished to take Konrad for my husband, instead of saying 'Yes', I answered with heartfelt zeal 'Of course!' Then we exchanged the rings and kissed, for the first time in public. The two mothers beamed with happiness; the shy old man incessantly wiggled his moustache and looked like a tender rabbit; an aunt sobbed her heart out.

Then we said goodbye to the relatives and, with Adam and Teresa, set off in one of the military cars for a little drive. Without asking anyone the middle-aged soldier driver took us to the outskirts of the town, straight to a vast forest. There we stopped, got out of the car and dived into the fragrant, green brake – just the two of us since Teresa and Adam immediately got lost in the trees. It was hot and close and clouds of gnats hovered in the still air, biting our arms and legs. A storm was brewing. The first huge drops of torrential rain forced us to run back to the open car.

When, soaked and stung but wonderfully happy, we finally arrived home, Zofia told us off sternly for having taken so long and having kept the guests waiting. A number of friends had arrived for the party and they all gathered round the beautifully laid table. Zofia had moved heaven and earth to produce a veritable feast – no easy feat in those days of post-war scarcity. She had even managed to get partridges – a luxury at the best of times!

Later, in the evening, to my surprise and delight, a little military band was sent in by the Colonel. The funiture was moved to the walls, the neighbours, lured by sound of music, arrived with bottles of vodka, and the best part of the party began. Back in my ordinary clothes, my hair in a happy mess, I whirled with my brand-new husband in a crazy dance. Family, friends, neighbours ceased to exist, as though we were dancing alone on the face of the earth.

Some time in the middle of this frantic night, it was noticed that the bridegroom's father had disappered and an anxious search began. He was finally found in the common loft, sleeping peacefully on his own sofa that had been moved from the tiny flat to make room for the party.

At last the visitors left. Zofia, exhausted after the hectic day, went to bed, and we were left alone in the room strewn with party debris. Working together for the first time, we made our nuptial bed that was in fact only Konrad's very narrow couch.

· 5 ·

The Post House Hotel on the outskirts of Leeds lies in a vast, slightly neglected park off the main road. It has an air of independence, as though it had little to do with the town itself. It is, in fact, just one of those big, modern hotels which pretend to be country havens. The reason why, in 1971, we chose this place to celebrate our wedding anniversary was that we had not yet found any other nice-looking place – it was only six weeks, after all, since we had arrived in Leeds. So we booked a table at the restaurant and spent a happy evening there. Since then we have always returned there on the eighteenth of August.

I do not remember when we first started celebrating our anniversaries by eating out. It must have been quite a few years after the wedding itself, in the late fifties, when the bitterly scarce time of the Six-Year-Economic Plan was over and we were well enough off to afford an occasional visit to a restaurant. Our favourite place then was the Bristol, once the best and grandest hotel in postwar Warsaw, dignified and solemn enough to add a touch of splendour and continuity to our annual celebrations. I vividly remember its spacious halls, their high ceilings stuccoed in Art Nouveau style; the crystal chandeliers ablaze with electric lights even in the midst of a sunny day and reflected in the magnificent mirrors; the deep velvet chairs; the tables covered with snow-white linen; the snow-white waiters who would never come when they were most needed and who answered you back if you complained. And what food they used to serve, despite the ailing economy of the socialist state! Plump herrings in sour cream that melted in the mouth like butter before being washed down with frosty vodka; golden crispy goose baked with apples and served with beetroots and red cabbage; shapely goblets heaped with vanilla ice-cream, fruit and crispy wafers . . . I would hurry off to the Bristol straight from work, sneaking out of my office much earlier than allowed despite strict socialist discipline: it added a touch of daring to the occasion. Konrad never needed to sneak out: at that time of year he was free from academic work. Our children would be safely away, packed off with a nanny somewhere in the country for the summer. So there was no need to hurry.

We have carried on our celebrations, year in, year out, never missing a single one, not even at the sad time of crisis that in the sixties threatened to wreck our marriage. It has always helped to talk and to listen.

Our life changed in every way when we left Poland but this ritual remained. We somehow took it with us and planted it out in another soil, another landscape.

. . . The stony terrace of an Old Jaffa restaurant overlooked clusters of haggard palm trees, the beach, the quiet sea at sunset. The dark, untidy boys served houmus with black olives, shashliks and grapefruit juice. Emaciated stray cats waited for their bits under the table. Flies hummed in the stifling air. In distress we talked about the unavoidable changes looming ahead and about our loved ones who we would have to leave behind: our newly married Lena, my mother who was getting old, Sophie dying from cancer . . .

We are sitting now in the bar of the Post House Hotel, thirty-odd years after our wedding. The subdued light and the soft tunes of the old-time songs make us feel very private. The creamy, furry fleece of Yorkshire sheep adorn the walls of the bar, a thick wall-to-wall carpet muffles the sounds of the steps. Sipping our ice-cold whiskies, we whisper.

Later, we shall sit in the restaurant at our favourite table by the window. Held together in the warm circle of the candlelight, we shall feel cut off from the outer world. If we look down into the darkening park, we may see, by chance, a group of young hares nibbling on the lawn. The smart, efficient waiter will softly appear and disappear, serving us delicacies with French-sounding names and a touch of English flavour.

But first, still in the bar, we talk. We talk about yet another year of our married life, and about our daughters. We try to sum up what has been good, what bad, and what should be better. We think about what must be done in the coming year, and about all the things we cannot prevent – missiles, rising unemployment, Israel's military ventures . . . In the past we used to plan our children's future. But this is over now that they live their own independent lives. So sitting in the bar we watch them tenderly from afar, telling each other that Lena copes so bravely with her work and her family on the edge of the Israeli volcano; that Monika works so hard and earns so little, while her first architectural project, an old people's home, has been such a success; that Sylvia, after all her years of queuing for the dole, is now so well thought of in London galleries and, though she still earns so little, does such fine work; that those who share our daughters' lives are good, hard-working men, loving and deserving love; that life has been kind to us if, after all those years, we still can sit peacefully together and talk and look forward to the year which is just beginning.

*

In the summer of 1948 major events were taking place in Poland. With suspicion between former allies now turning into hostility of cold war, Stalin was anxious to tighten the screw and gain full control over the satellite states. At the end of August, just a couple of days before the honeymoon that we had planned so carefully, Konrad was ordered to postpone his leave and to stay in his unit until further notice. A plenary meeting of the Central Committee of the Polish Workers' Party was in session and there were rumours that the party leader, Gomułka, and his close associates were in deep trouble for 'right wing deviation'. A major purge was expected in the party ranks and was bringing to a head a host of simmering and unresolved conflicts. The army was therefore put on the alert and all officers' leave temporarily called off.

It was too late to change our plans: a room in a pension in the mountains had been booked for September and it was impossible to postpone it till later. Konrad begged me to go on my own. He hoped to join me very soon. So, there I was, all alone on a train going on my honeymoon. And then all alone, for a whole week in a double-bed hotel room. I had to fend off numerous romantic advances from other holiday-makers. My wedding ring served as my shield and my weapon.

At last Konrad arrived, more handsome than ever, and we still had three weeks of our honeymoon left. It was the most wonderful time of our life. We explored the unfamiliar western mountains and the beautiful villages that had recently been acquired by Poland in her postwar 'shift to the West'. Our boundless bliss did not last long, however. On the fourteenth day Konrad received a wire ordering him to return to his unit at once. He never told me the reason for this urgent recall and I never asked him. He might have told me if I had been a member of the Party. Since I was not, we always tried to avoid talking about any secret State or Party matters.

I went back to my new Warsaw home, brought suddenly from heaven to earth. Konrad was away every day from early morning till late at night and often missed his university lectures. At night, when we were at last together, his parents had to pass through our room on their way to the bathroom.

Housework and studying were not enough for me. I urgently needed a job. Konrad no longer objected – we had made an uneasy agreement about it before our wedding.

It was very easy to get a job in the late 1940s. Hands and brains were needed not only at building sites and in the factories and steelworks – they were also urgently in demand at the new offices, headquarters and institutes mushrooming under the new regime, with its desire to administer every aspect of national life. Jobs chased people, age or lack of skills being no bar. For young, intelligent men and women with clean political records and a willingness to learn new skills, the sky was the limit. They could choose almost any job they wished and could be sure of rapid promotion.

Now, when I think about my twins' uphill struggle to find work after they had both acquired high professional qualifications, about all those endless application forms they had to fill and all those interviews they attended, about all those heart-breaking rejections and long periods of despair, I see how lucky I had been in the other days.

Three weeks after my return from the mountains I was already deep in a new job that I had found by chance. Adam had a disconcerting habit of changing his girlfriends very frequently – each time we met I had to be friendly to a totally new person, which I found very difficult. One Sunday, he called in with Barbara, a serious-looking person in her thirties. She was a Party member and had a responsible job as personnel officer at the headquarters of the state-run Film Polski*. Having heard I was looking for work she expounded at length on the prestige and fascination of working in this field. I did not need much persuading. The thing I most dreaded was working in a boring job, an office like the Fish Industry Head Office or the General Management of Milk Bars. So anything to do with films, no matter what kind of work, seemed thrilling to me. Besides, Film Polski was in Pulawska Street, ten minutes' walk from home.

Barbara moved fast and fixed an appointment for me with the director of the personnel department on the following Wednesday. The interview took place in a smart office furnished with leather armchairs and an impressive mahogany desk, and lasted only a few minutes. The director asked me a few questions about my education and work experience and offered me a clerical job in the finance department. It was exactly the kind of work I feared, but since it had something to do with films, I accepted at once. However, I returned home very disappointed.

At eight o'clock the following Monday, I reported to the same

* Polish Film

director and was introduced by him to the head of the Finance Department. But then, all of a sudden, he said he had changed his mind and had decided I would fit in better in the Programme Department. They needed a secretary, he said. But first I must talk to the Programme director.

This turned out to be a tall, good-looking and very well-dressed woman in her late thirties. Only some time later did I learn that she was the wife of one of the most feared men in the country – the man in charge of public security. The sound of her name was enough to make many citizens tremble, but this was not the only reason why she commanded respect: competent, efficient and domineering, Diana was a powerful personality in her own right. I felt this at once as she greeted me, politely but with a marked distance. This time I was asked about my general interests, whether I had seen any films recently released and what I thought of them. Since I was very keen on films and hardly ever missed a new one, I started speaking fluently and with pleasure. Diana listened attentively but after a while broke in and asked me to go straight to my desk as the previous secretary had left three days ago and there were a lot of letters waiting to be typed.

I sat in a little room between the director's office and a big room occupied by the rest of the staff, trying to decipher the unfamiliar handwriting of my new superiors. Two deputy directors provided most of the mail. One of them was the wife of the editor-in-chief of a literary weekly, the other was a general's wife: the budding red bourgeoisie, an offspring of the new social deal. They were both well groomed and elegantly dressed, but their writing left plenty of room for improvement. Typing their letters I could not resist the temptation to change words and rephrase what they had said. Later, when I submitted the typed letters to Diana for signing, she glanced at me oddly while reading them but said nothing.

Barbara called at my office to congratulate me on the job. She brought the contract I had to sign. Only on reading this did I learn what my salary was to be: I had forgotten to ask about it at the interview. It was very low, in fact – only a few zloties per month more than I had earned as a typist. I was classified as grade eleven on the pay scale, one grade higher than a typist and two grades higher than the departmental storekeeper who was at the bottom of the scale.

On Tuesday Diana said I should leave my letters for a while because there was something more urgent to be done – some work on a long article about the new Polish film called *The Fair Fields**. The film was nearly finished and would be appearing on the screens early the following year. Like any other film, Diana explained, it needed publicity material to stimulate public interest and help the viewer understand the central ideas of the film. The text that had been done was very poorly written and she wanted me to try and improve it.

I started work enthusiastically and read all about the exploitation of poor peasants by the rich; about land reform and the important task of electrification in the countryside; about the enemies of democratic Poland who could not tolerate our great achievements and retaliated with sabotage. Not having seen the film itself, it was hard to know what to do with the text. I asked one of my new colleagues for help and he gave me the script of the film. Alas, this was not much better than the article. So I was left to my own resources. In desperation I used my imagination and completely rewrote the article. Proud of my creation I handed it over to Diana before the end of my second working day. (Much later, when *The Fair Fields* appeared in Warsaw cinemas, I discovered that all my work had been in vain – the film was very poor and the cinemas were almost empty.)

On the third day, my boss told me that she was looking for a new secretary and would I like the post of junior programme officer? This meant quite a promotion – from grade eleven up to grade nine.

I was moved from the little room to the big one. Now there was a chance I might get to know my colleagues and their work. Apart from the two deputy directors who seemed to do very little, all the staff worked very hard indeed. A harassed young woman hung on the telephone all day shouting instructions to the

* Jasne Łany

· 63 ·

producers at the film studio in Łódź (the only studio at the time), ordering copies of films in production, giving numbers and dates, asking about costs and technical details which I could hardly understand. Only now and then did she leave the telephone to tell the storekeeper which copies he had to deliver, where and when. The publicity manager, a jovial young man called Zbigniew, was constantly on the move, going out, coming back, fussing over heaps of proofs or sketches and talking at his desk to artists and writers who were working on posters and publicity material for new films. (One of them was the author of the article I had worked on a day before.) Mrs Krasnopolska, a friendly, ever-smiling person from a dispossessed aristocratic family, typed non-stop, her eyes fixed on foreign texts. She earned her living by translating French, German and English dialogue into Polish for the foreign films bought for Polish screening. The office had an atmosphere of bustle and of great commitment to an important cause. I watched my colleagues with passionate admiration: theirs was the kind of life I had always longed for. I yearned to be one of them.

My own work was much less strenuous, though no less exciting. I had to report on foreign films that might be bought by Film Polski, and to provide detailed descriptions and comments. Many foreign films arrived daily and the decision makers were too busy to see them all. My summaries and comments were meant to help them make a first selection.

I now spent most of my time in a little projection room on the fifth floor watching one film after another, sometimes four in a day. Sitting alone in the cosy darkness and knowing that the films were being shown for me alone was great fun in itself, to say nothing of the rare chance to see new films from all over the world. Who else in democratic Poland was able to watch such a wide range of unscreened pictures from the West just as they came, whether 'good' or 'bad' for public morale? I enjoyed myself enormously, even when the films were bad – there was a lot of Hollywood and international rubbish alongside the best films of the late forties. I saw the great pictures of Italian neo-realism; French dramas and comedies by directors such as Claude Autant-

Lara, Marcel Carné, René Clair, René Clément, Jules Dassin, Jean Renoir; British films like *It Always Rains on Sunday* – an example of early English realism, like *Hamlet* with Laurence Olivier, *Great Expectations* and *Oliver Twist* directed by David Lean, and the two powerful dramas directed by Carol Reed: *The Third Man* with Orson Welles and *Odd Man Out* with James Mason as an IRA man on the run.

I was very happy at this early stage of my film career. My only sadness was that Konrad, an even greater film enthusiast than myself, could not sit next to me in the sweet darkness of the projection room and share my pleasure.

Being a student I was allowed to stop work an hour earlier than anyone else. I badly needed this time for my studies. Every afternoon at three o'clock I hurried from Pulawska Street straight to the other end of town without even stopping to eat – I could spare no time for meals in the canteen.

As if my exciting job, my studies and the joy of my married life were not enough, I decided to join ZMP – the Union of Polish Youth. This Union had been created shortly before through the merger of a number of youth organisations. Its declared aim was to unite young people of all social and political backgrounds who wished to promote the cause of internationalism and socialism; to involve them in the struggle for national reconstruction and in the work for national prosperity and social justice. A number of people I knew and trusted had joined ZMP. I decided it was the right place for me too. I had had enough of standing outside keeping myself aloof; I wanted to act, to be useful, to belong.

The academic branch of ZMP that I joined had its own, academic ways of promoting the aims of the organisation. To my delight, I was given the job of writing film reviews for the weekly student paper and I was very happy to do this alongside my official work. My task was to look at the films I reviewed from a particular point of view: to determine whether and how the film helped to raise the socialist consciousness of the audience. Since I only reviewed films that were already being shown, most of them were Soviet and this made my task only too easy. But practice turns into habit, habit into nature and little by little, without giving it much thought, I began to see in the films only what I was expected to look for. The political message of the film became more important to me than its artistic value.

Soon after I started working, our family life underwent a major change. Zofia decided to follow in my footsteps and get herself a full-time job. Ambitious and capable, full of strength and energy despite her poor health (she had been a diabetic for as long as she could remember), she disliked the idea of being the only person in the family not going out to work. She strongly resented having to slave at home cooking, cleaning and washing for the three wage-earners. Her husband and son tried at first to dissuade her, but I fully supported the idea: I understood how she felt and respected her decision.

Finding a good job was even easier for Zofia than for myself. With excellent references from her work in the Soviet Union, her Party card and majestic appearance, she was immediately offered a job as manageress of one of the biggest and grandest restaurants in Warsaw. Now all four of us left home early each morning and returned late, tired but full of tales of the past day to tell at the supper table.

Though she worked eight hours a day, Zofia continued as head of the household. All daily housework she turned over to a maid she had brought home after her first day at work. She was a country girl who had left her village and come to Warsaw looking for a job. Attracted by the city life-style and the vast new opportunities for employment in industry, crowds of young people were pouring into the capital from the country. There was always work waiting for them but there were major problems in finding somewhere to live. Many a girl would gladly accept work as a domestic servant, at least to start with. This was the case with our new maid who seemed to be delighted when she was offered a folding bed to sleep on in the kitchen at night. She turned out to be good and efficient at everything she did. In fact, she was too good. After a month Zofia decided it was a crime to exploit her as a servant and offered her a more dignified job together with a place to sleep in the restaurant she ran. After that a long succession of country girls came and went, none staying with us for longer than a few months before being launched into a better life by Zofia. None was as good as the first one, some were not good at all, but Zofia kept her beady eyes on everything and it somehow worked. I could with a clear conscience ignore all daily household tasks.

It is hard for me now to see how, with such a full and busy life, Konrad and I were still able to find time to enjoy ourselves together. But the truth is we did. We had lots of friends, mainly Konrad's fellow officers and their wives, who were always ready to go out, to throw a party or attend one. We loved dancing; we rushed to see every new play in the Warsaw theatres – new theatres opened all the time – and we adored concerts. Konrad was a great football fan, so we rarely missed any international match. But more than anything else, we were fond of films, and I was quite happy to spend all evening in the cinema after having seen three or four films during the day.

It was a very happy, carefree time. All these years later I still remember it as such, though I now know that it was then that the seeds of future disasters were being sown. As we worked, studied and danced, the iron hand of Stalin was tightening around our necks, helped by our own hard work and youthful enthusiasm.

Four months after I started working in the Programme Department, Zbigniew, the publicity manager, moved to a better paid job in the steel industry. His job was offered to me.

So now I was publicity manager – grade seven on the pay list. I immersed myself in my new work with more frenzy than ever. But it was very hard. Naturally shy, I felt terribly uneasy about being in a position of authority over the prominent writers and artists from whom I had to commission articles and posters. I hated having to give them instructions, and even more having to ask for alterations before accepting their work. I had to constantly get everyone to hurry up, including myself; every poster and programme was needed for yesterday. I got very upset if Diana told me off for missing a deadline. I stopped going to lectures and became withdrawn and short-tempered at home. I was living under great stress, and it was some time before I could cope with my new social self.

Then, at the beginning of April 1949, I realised I was pregnant. Konrad and I had never thought of having a baby so soon. We were still young – I was not yet twenty-three, Konrad only nine months older. He was born the night I was conceived and always claimed that the first thing he did after arriving in this world was to order himself a suitable wife. Our busy life felt so precariously balanced that anything extra, however small, could have wrecked the balance. We had never properly discussed the subject of children: we had taken it for granted we would have a baby when we'd finished our studies. We did what we could to avoid my getting pregnant, but there was not much one could do in Poland in the late 1940s: family planning did not exist, reliable contraceptives were not available, and home-made devices were a game of chance. Thank heaven for it: that was how Lena was conceived.

The clear realisation that I was pregnant came to me one day when I was listening to a concert. It was one of the musical matinees we often went to on Sundays. On that particular day the Warsaw Philharmonic Orchestra and Choir were performing Prokofiev's oratorio, *Alexander Nevski*. The monumental music made me forget all my daily worries and sink deep into my innermost thoughts. Suddenly, I knew it beyond any doubt: I was expecting a child. A strong, warm wave of peaceful joy descended over me with the powerful music. I felt I had longed for this child for years. I knew that, come what may, Konrad would be happy too.

His response to the news, which I told him as soon as we left the concert hall, surpassed all my expectations. He danced wildly in the street and kissed me right there, causing a public sensation. I had great trouble in convincing him that I could still walk and did not need a taxi. Despite his captain's rank, he was still a boy.

At the start of the happy times that were to follow, I had to resist great pressure from my doctor uncles to terminate the pregnancy because of my TB. They said the illness, which had clearly been recently receding, might strike again with increased vigour now that I was pregnant. Other people strongly advised against giving birth to children at all now that the cold war was growing more serious hour by hour and another world war seemed imminent. I would not listen. I decided to take my child's destiny into my own hands. My family backed me up. Mother, who worried constantly about my health, did not think that having a baby could do me any harm. She was proved right. My in-laws longed for a grandchild and did all they could to keep me fit and healthy. Zofia fed me with oranges from some secret source – they were never available in the shops. My father-in-law would queue for hours after a day of hard work to get me fresh butter. My colleagues at work were very considerate and Diana, a devoted mother herself, took me under her wing. To save me from lifting loads of printed material and photos and from climbing up to high shelves, she immediately found me a young male assistant to do all the hard work.

But I was worried. I knew that my job as a publicity manager was coming to an end: it could not be kept open till my return. I expected to be away for twelve weeks maternity leave, during which time someone else would have to be appointed to do my work. Diana promised to find me another job in the department when I came back.

The law required me to begin my leave two weeks before the expected date of delivery. But I decided to continue working as long as I could in order to save my time off for being with the baby. Since I felt fit and had special privileges, I managed to stay at work till the very last day. On 15 November, late at night, Konrad took me to the military hospital and on the following day my first daughter, Lena, arrived happily in a bleak, wet, autumnal world.

· 6 ·

Another bleak, wet, autumnal day, this time November 1984. The garden outside the bay window is shrouded in drizzle, the lawn strewn with golden leaves. The bare, almost black branches of the beech tree stand out in sharp contrast against the pale sky. Only the roses – red, creamy and bright yellow – seem to thrive in this gloom on the verge of winter: it's England.

Lena, thirty-five today, has shut herself away in the dining-room to work on her thesis. This is why she has come all the way from Jerusalem: to sit alone in the tranquillity of this cosy room, not to be interrupted, to work. This is the only place in the world where she can forget her daily responsibilities and be a child again away from her own children; to be caressed, spoiled and cared for. For three weeks at least, three short, peaceful weeks.

Sitting idly in front of my typewriter I think about her future. How will she remember her present life when she is my age? Will she remember that at the time as she struggled through the most difficult parts of her doctoral project, the newly elected Israeli government entered upon a desperate fight against inflation which had just reached 450 per cent? How strangely our memory works, how easily it pushes away matters of public importance and makes space for petty joys and sorrows! After thirty-five years I can still clearly remember how, aching with pain and thirst in labour, I craved for juicy grapes, and how Konrad sent me some hard, sour apples instead because no other fruit was then available. I shall never forget this. But what was happening in Poland at the very same time? Let's push the typewriter aside and consult a book on the history of the Polish People's Republic.

November 1949 was . . . a turning point for the PZPR*
and for Poland itself. The Third Plenum of the Central
Committee, which met from 11 to 13 November . . . called
for an inquiry into the past of all men in responsible
positions, for a purge of unreliable elements from the
PZPR, for recruitment to the Party from among workers
and peasants, and for constant vigilance of Party members
against the class enemies . . .

The call for vigilance . . . did have far-reaching effects . . .
The purge did not stop at the Party. The army, central and
co-operative and social organisations lost thousands of
competent men because their backgrounds aroused
suspicion as to their loyalty. Gentry, bourgeois or
prosperous peasant origin was fatal. Anybody connected
with the prewar regime, one of the prewar parties, the
London government-in-exile, or of the pro-'London'
underground was automatically disqualified. Family ties
with someone who had once offended the Party or lived in
the West were often enough to disqualify a man from
holding a responsible position . . . Many places were filled
by Party activists who had no formal qualifications for them
. . . The campaign of 'vigilance' and the theory that the
capitalist world sought to subvert communist systems from
within led to a vast increase in the size and activity of the
security police after November 1949. It was an organisation
of full-time professionals skilled in uncovering spies and
saboteurs . . . The cases brought to light by the security
police were based upon fabricated evidence or confessions
extracted by torture . . .

A network of secret agents, often disguised as 'personnel
officers' in factories and offices, was constructed,

---

* Polska Zjednoczona Partia Robotnicza – Polish United Workers' Party.

supplemented by a large number of unpaid informers
recruited by blackmail or ideological appeal.*

*

When after my maternity leave, filled to the brim with new joys
and new domestic responsibilities, I left my twelve-week-old
Lena at the mercy of our current maid and returned to work, I
found the Programme Department changed beyond recognition.
Several of my colleagues had left and had been replaced by
strangers. There was also a new director – Diana had been
promoted to the more prestigious post of director to the newly
created Film Export and Import Office. She had not forgotten
me, though – she had left a message with Barbara telling me to
get in touch with her as soon as I got back.

Worried and nervous, I took a tram to her new office in the city
centre and reported to the director's secretary. I was told it was
impossible to see Diana either today or tomorrow as she was
terribly busy. But the secretary knew my 'case', and said I should
get in touch straight away with the personnel manager as there
was a job waiting for me.

Manager Barski was a middle-aged man with a bushy moustache and restless eyes. He got up as I entered his office and left
his desk to shake both of my hands cordially. 'Welcome, welcome,
comrade,' he called me – a sign of special benevolence since I was
not a Party member. He said they were all very pleased that I was
going to join their team, though I had no idea who 'they' were.
They had heard a lot about me, he continued, only the best, only
the best indeed, as far as my skills and my truly socialist attitude to
work were concerned. Somehow he knew I was a member of the
students' ZMP organisation, although I had never talked about
my student life at work. He informed me that he was the deputy
secretary of the Party organisation in 'our' office and expressed his
hope for 'our' fruitful co-operation. Somewhat puzzled, yet very

* *The History of Poland since 1863*, edited by R.F. Leslie, Cambridge University
Press, 1980, p. 304–307.

pleased by such a warm welcome, I began gradually to feel less tense and anxious: a job was waiting for me, people I did not know about knew about me and respected me in advance. I could not wait to start working.

In the big, dark office four people were busy at their desks: two old ladies around fifty who looked a bit *ancien regime*, a man in his thirties, and a dark girl glued to her typewriter. They were all fluent in foreign languages and their work had something to do with this, but exactly what I cannot remember. My work, it turned out, required foreign languages too. One of the old ladies, who introduced herself as my boss, handed me a big pile of French and Russian magazines. My job was to look through them, find any film reviews and articles on the cinema and then translate them into Polish, or just summarise them for an internal monthly bulletin. It was pleasant work. I knew French very well and my knowledge of Russian, which I had picked up in childhood from my Russian-born grandmother and later considerably improved due to the compulsory classes at the Academy, was just sufficient to understand the articles with the aid of a dictionary. But there was no charm in this work, no reason to hurry with it, no feeling of committing myself to an important cause. My new colleagues worked in silence, glued to their desks, seldom talking to each other. They looked bored and indifferent, and so was I.

I worked in silence for seven hours a day, allowed off the last hour as a young mother and a student. I then rushed home to see my poor, deserted child, missing most of my lectures. Every day as I started tidying my desk at three o'clock, I caught critical glances and the hostile whispers from the two old ladies. They strongly disapproved of combining motherhood with studies and work, it would have been unthinkable in their day.

Very soon I made friends with Jacqueline, the typist. She was the same age as myself, a beautiful girl, half French. She had been born in France and had lived there until her French father died. Only then, quite recently, had she come with her Polish mother to live in Warsaw. Both her parents had been members of the French Communist Party and had fought in the French Resistance during the war. Jacqueline was clever, bilingual and very left wing in her views. Despite her convictions, however, she was not at all happy with things in Poland and often complained that life in Warsaw was dull and drab by comparison with Paris. Like myself, she found her work boring and strongly resented the two 'aristocrats', as she called our senior colleagues. Whenever we could we sneaked out of the room and had a private chat in the corridor. It helped us bear it all.

Diana I saw only very rarely, and when I did there was no chance of talking to her privately. The distance between us had grown considerably: she was now the head of a big, important office with dozens of employees and had no time for individuals. I began to appreciate all the more the open friendly way in which the personnel manager Barski spoke to me whenever we came across each other. Once, having met me in the corridor, he invited me to his office. He said he could see I was not happy with my work and he wanted to know why. I confessed that I found it very unsatisfying to work on matters of little importance, especially those which had no emotional meaning to me. He nodded understandingly and warmly squeezed my hand. There were lots of important things I could do to help the Party, he said. We had just embarked upon the decisive battle of the Six Year Plan, we were striving to change Poland from a backward, agricultural country into an industrial one; we were fighting for higher living standards for the people, for the growth of national culture. But in order to achieve these aims, he stressed, in order to build a happy future, we had to work hard and put up with many shortcomings in this transitory stage. Yet, he sighed, there were people, many people in our country who could not or did not want to understand the need for sacrifice.

Barski stopped and looked deep into my eyes. The Party, he said, needed young, intelligent, enthusiastic people ready to explain its aims to those who could not see the wood for the trees. I listened intently. I felt he was just about to show me the way to a life of great deeds and commitment, a life I had been longing for. And sure enough, from matters of general importance he quickly turned to my own 'case'. In a slightly solemn way he assured me that the Party organisation, as well as he himself, trusted me and therefore, though I was not a Party member, wanted to offer me the honourable function of an agitator. This meant talking to people, explaining things and answering questions – questions that would sometimes be hard to answer. I could always come back and ask him for advice if I needed it, he said. He gave me a notebook with the words 'Diary of an Agitator' printed on its cover in which I should keep a record of my conversations, of questions asked and answers given, of the arguments and counter-arguments of the people I might be talking to. Flattered, bubbling with enthusiasm and happy that I had found an outlet for my beloved writing, I grabbed the notebook and promised to do my best.

Though I had never been particularly keen on talking about politics, Barski's appeal and the promise I had given him prompt-ed me to take any opportunity for political discussions or even to start them myself. I began to answer back the old ladies when they grumbled about 'the good old days'; I argued with my gentleman colleague about the deep ideological values of some second-rate Soviet film; I chastised Jacqueline for her complaints about the lack of nylon stockings in the shops when the whole nation was making such an effort to build the giant steel works at Nowa Huta. I felt tempted to tell Jacqueline that I had been honoured with the function of an agitator – being a sincere Communist she would surely have been most approving. But Barski had stressed that I must keep my mission secret, so I told her nothing.

I duly kept a record of my conversations and my notebook quickly filled up with juicy descriptions of people and their views. After a month or so, Barski invited me to his office again to ask how I was getting on with my assignment. I showed him the notebook and he read it through in my presence, smiling from time to time and making witty remarks. When he had finished, he returned the notebook to me. 'Splendid, splendid, comrade,' he said. 'Please continue, And, dear comrade, if you ever consider applying for party membership, I would be happy to recommend you most highly. Very happy indeed.'

Although I did not consider joining the Party, I felt very

proud. I could not wait to tell Konrad what had happened to me. I knew he would be very proud of me, too. Since I had met him and fallen in love with him, a wish to make him happy and proud of me always lay behind everything I did and added special meaning to my achievements.

Having a young baby whom I was breast-feeding three times a day – once in the morning and twice after work – I had to stop going to lectures and studied on my own when Lena was asleep. For this reason I had also left the academic ZMP organisation and joined the non-academic one at work. It was a small organisation: three or four young typists including Jacqueline, two messenger boys, some junior clerks and a projectionist. The head of the organisation, Zubrowski, was an assistant accountant from the finance department, a pale, thin young man whose eyes burnt with the unshakable faith of a prophet. At meetings he made desperate attempts to warm up the rather sluggish participants, of whom Jacqueline was by far the most alert and keen. The usual subjects of discussion at the meetings were current political and economic events, and daily problems that the ZMP organisation should be helping to solve. Soon after my second talk with Barski, the ZMP meeting took an unexpected turn. His eyes ablaze with wrath, his voice rising to its highest pitch, Zubrowski publicly accused Jacqueline of being an advocate of anti-socialist ideas and a well-disguised mouthpiece for hostile Western propaganda. Reading from some notes in front of him, he quoted Jacqueline's alleged utterances about the drabness of Polish life and the superiority of French shops. I listened amazed. I couldn't understand how Zubrowski had come to know what Jacqueline thought, and how he could possibly reach his preposterous conclusions on the basis of her innocent grumblings. She sat next to me, utterly aghast, pale and breathless. Zubrowski went on with his accusations. Suddenly, like a bolt from the blue, some words of his fiery speech struck a familiar chord: yes, beyond any doubt he was quoting words that Jacqueline had once spoken when talking to me and which I had duly recorded in my notebook. On an impulse, I grasped her hand, but she wrenched it furiously from my grip. She stared at me with anger and contempt.

On a motion of Zubrowski's Jacqueline was expelled at the end of the meeting from the ranks of the ZMP. All but myself voted weakly in favour. I made an awkward attempt to speak up in her defence but to no avail. Later she turned her back on me as I tried desperately to explain what had happened. She never came to work again. Shattered and betrayed, she resigned and disappeared from my life for ever.

I was left on my own with an unbearable burden of guilt and shame. Konrad was the only person I could turn to. He was deeply shaken when he heard the story. He sank deep into uneasy thoughts. He was devastated for Jacqueline but obviously for me too. He said it was a deplorable mistake to have told Barski what I knew about my colleagues. He was clearly not a man to be trusted. Unfortunately, Konrad explained, the Party ranks were still full of untrustworthy individuals, ruthlessly ambitious climbers and ideologically immature members. Yet, despite this transitory weakness, despite the grave mistakes often committed in its name, the Party was the most powerful agent of social justice and had to be implicitly trusted. You cannot make an omelette, he said, without breaking eggs. You cannot make a revolution without accidentally hurting some of the innocent. The Soviet Revolution had created many victims and there had been many mistakes. Casualties could occur in our far less bloody Polish revolution too. Jacqueline was one of them. It was heart-breaking, but we had to put up with such things if we wanted to fight for a better world.

I understood the theory. It did not help me, however, to come to terms with my guilt and with the injustice done. My days at work became an ordeal. I could hardly bear the sight of Jacqueline's deserted desk. I did not dare venture into the corridor lest I came face to face with Barski.

Summer was coming. Lena and the maid were sent into the country near Warsaw. I commuted every day after work to Michalin to spend some time with her, to feed her once a day at least, then bath her and put her to bed. Late at night I returned home. Soon after the Jacqueline affair I felt I could bear my work no longer and applied for my statutory one-month holiday. It was instantly granted. Before leaving, I dropped Diana a line. I told her that I was disappointed with my work and asked her to help me find something more interesting in the same field.

Michalin was a little place in the woods, with little wooden houses scattered among old pine-trees. We had rented one of the houses for the whole summer and there I buried myself with my child and my shame. I sent the maid back to Warsaw, deciding to devote all my time and thoughts to my little girl whom I had recently neglected.

Though Michalin was very near Warsaw, I found myself virtually cut off from the outside world. I lived in the cottage alone with my baby, without a radio or a telephone; there was not a soul in the immediate neighbourhood. Every couple of days I set off with Lena in her pram to the centre of the tiny village to do some shopping and buy newspapers that now became my only link with the world beyond the woods.

One day, shortly after arriving in Michalin, I read in the papers about the war which had just broken out between North and South Korea and which was soon to involve American forces. The shelves in the few shabby shops in the village were already almost empty and panic-stricken people were queuing for what dry noodles and soap there were left. A new world war seemed imminent.

*

Strange are the ways of memory. Today I can hardly remember how the Korean war started or when it came to an end. But I do remember my fear. Why do I stay calm now when the whole world dreads a new war? Why does my blood not run cold when I hear that a Cruise missile has now been stationed in this country? Why do I have this quiet, firm belief that we are safe on this little island – Konrad, myself and the twins – for as long as we live? It must be, I think, a complete failure of my imagination – as though my mind had frozen forty-odd years ago and now flatly refused to conjure up something worse than the Second World War: a universal disaster. I read papers, I watch TV, I've seen

The Day After and *Threads*, but none of this affects me: I still go on with my plans and hopes and never stop to think 'Why bother?' There is no fear deep in my soul, it is as though my whole ability to feel fear was exhausted then. I know I'll never see Nazi uniforms again; I know their planes will never drop bombs on my defenceless home; I know we shall never be put to death for being what we are – not in this country. So I sleep peacefully at night, safe in a deep conviction that, if the worst comes after all, we won't be singled out; and that, with a bit of luck, we may never live to see a nuclear winter.

*

In the summer of 1950, my fear was still alive, my imagination vivid. The horror I had experienced when young now returned with renewed vigour: there was my tiny child to fear for, there was my husband. He had already been put on alert and had sent me a message saying he could not come, not even for a short visit. The warm, peaceful days of my seclusion, serenaded by the whispers of the pine trees and Lena's joyful cooing, turned into a nightmare. Seized by a claw of fear I waited for disaster.

Just at the end of my leave Lena caught measles and I had to stay on with her for the following month, this time on maternity sick leave. The summer was nearly over when we finally returned to Warsaw. In the meantime the Korean war had ceased to be news. As usually happens with wars that rage somewhere far away and do not affect our daily lives, people had got used to the press reports and had stopped panicking.

A great surprise was waiting for me on my return. While I was away, Konrad had found a better flat – one that had just come empty in the same building. It had three rooms instead of two, so now at last we could live comfortably, with no need to share our bedroom with Lena. Konrad's parents were better off too, they no longer had to walk through our room. Konrad had also been promoted to a higher rank – he had become one of the youngest majors in the Polish army. Some simpletons in the neighbourhood now called me 'Mrs Major'.

But the best thing that happened to me that autumn was that I was offered a new job and did not have to return to my previous loathsome work. Though nobody ever said so, I knew it was Diana again who was behind this offer. She had left the Film Export and Import office and had moved on to a still more responsible job as deputy director of a big film studio which had just been built in Warsaw to produce documentary films. And I was invited to work there, too. So, in October 1950, I entered an entirely new world which I still remember as the best one I ever worked in – the only job in my long working life that gave me a chance to fulfil my greatest dreams: a world of creative work, of passionate devotion, of ambitious projects and endless excitement. The premises of the Documentary Film Studio were totally different from the city blocks and drab offices where I had worked before. It was situated out of the city centre on a large plot of land surrounded by a wall with a guarded gate. A low, flat but spacious building occupied the centre of the open space and housed the different departments involved in actual film production: the studios, the laboratories, the montage workshops and sound recording rooms, the film stores and projection halls. The offices, library, press archives and editorial rooms nestled in cheerful green wooden huts that popped up from among thick bushes all over the place. It felt like being in the country, full of space, light and fresh air, far away from the dry and dusty world of offices. There was a feeling of great adventure in the air, an atmosphere of romance – or perhaps it was just my own romantic nature that made it feel like that to me. People wandered to and fro, to the main building and back, from one hut to another, meeting on their way and stopping for a brief chat. Some of them were well known, some famous: actors, writers and composers, cameramen and journalists who had served in the army during the war and had reported direct from the front. They now formed the core of the newly born Polish documentary film industry. There were people whose voices and names I knew well from the weekly newsreels that were shown all over the country before every cinema performance. Cinema was then the most popular form of entertainment, able to reach far and wide, and the newsreels were very highly thought of, even by those who disliked their political slant and unquestioning commitment to the cause of building socialism in Poland. The team who produced the newsreels were very good: they avoided explicit propaganda as much as they could, chose interesting and varied topics, shot them well and provided sharp, witty commentary read by the best actors. The head of the team was a woman, as small as a child, plain and of indefinable age – a female Napoleon in charge of a little army of editors and cameramen. Natalia must have been a genius. I admired her only from a distance, since, despite my hopes, I never worked for her. Later, however, she played an important part in my life.

My job was to translate foreign documentary film commentaries into Polish, to commission other translators, and then to supervise the recording. Though I had three bosses over me – the chief editor, the deputy director and the head of the studio – I was fairly independent in my own field. I needed only to get their approval for the lines I wanted to record, and their signature on contracts with people I commissioned work from. My office was in one of the cosy huts. I shared it with three other editors, all of them women, all working in a different field, with no seniors or juniors amongst us except for a secretary and a typist who worked equally for all of us. We were all in our twenties with more or less similar skills and views. I quickly made friends with my new colleagues and felt that I had finally found the world I belonged to.

My family life also improved greatly at that time. With a bigger flat and slightly better salaries, Konrad and I decided to get a proper nanny for Lena. My mother said she would look for one and soon arrived with a friendly, experienced middle-aged woman who took to Lena at first sight and whom Lena seemed to like as well. On the day that Pani Waczkowska moved into our flat and took over all responsibility for the baby, as well as for shopping, cooking and cleaning, I heaved a sigh of relief. My child was now in the tender loving care of three people close to her – her nanny and her grandparents. My mother also was often around, and it was clear that Lena, even if her parents were often absent, was thriving in the warmth that only true love can bring.

So I plunged happily deep into my work, devoting most of my time and thoughts to the films I worked on and the people I worked with, meeting authors, spending long hours at the montage desk, helping actors in the recording studio – often till late at night.

I was also determined to continue my studies. We were now in the last year of the first degree course but I was very behind, having missed part of the previous year. This meant I had to take individual exams alongside keeping up with the current programme. It was hard and my results were poor. But I did manage to pass the exams I took. Konrad was now far ahead of me and little by little an intellectual gap was beginning to grow between us. But this did not affect our relationship – the more I became involved in the world outside our home, the stronger his respect for me and our mutual understanding grew. Konrad was really proud of me now – despite all my commitments, I even managed to be active in the ZMP.

The youth organisation in the Studio was quite unlike those I had belonged to earlier. It was a large and thriving organisation. Most of the members were bright and committed and really believed in what they were doing. I joined enthusiastically and was soon given my first assignment.

One Sunday a large ZMP team was going to a little village in the country to talk to local people about the benefits of collective farming and to offer any help they might need. I knew very little about farming and even less about collective farms. I wondered whether I had anything to offer. But the team leader, who had put my name on the list of activists, assured me that there was no need to worry: he was an experienced Party member, he would do most of the talking himself and tell us all what to do.

Early on Sunday morning we set off in the studio van, a dozen young men and women dressed in green shirts and red ties. It was still dark, the van jolted along, bouncing over the pot-holes of the narrow country roads. Happy and excited by our unusual adventure we sang as we went – mainly popular songs, praising work and youth. Wojtek Gruda, the team leader, was sitting next to me and when the singing stopped we began to talk. Fair-haired, blue-eyed and rather frail, he was not yet thirty, but he had already lived a very full life and had many stories to tell. He was born and brought up in a poor farming family in the east of Poland. He joined the Polish army as soon as it was formed in exile in Russia during the war. He received most of his education in the army and fought the Germans till the end of the war. Later he was discharged on grounds of poor health and, being a respected member of the Party, was given a series of important civilian posts. Now he was married, had two children and was personnel manager at the studio. His Party duties were to advise the ZMP.

No one was about when we arrived at the village – it seemed they were all at Sunday service in the church. We stopped at the village school, deserted on a Sunday but unlocked. As it was bitterly cold outdoors, we walked in. The school looked filthy. The walls, floors and desks in the little classrooms were thick with dirt and covered with ink stains; the windows so grimy that it was quite dark. It seemed a shame to waste our time, and anyway it was too cold to sit doing nothing, so Wojtek suggested we clean the place while we waited. We found some buckets and brushes in the corridor and set to work enthusiastically. Meantime Wojtek went off to the church to look for the head of the local council. When he returned at noon, all the ink had been cleaned off the walls and desks, the floors were neatly scrubbed and sunshine streamed into the classrooms through spotless window panes. Wojtek congratulated us on our work. He was pleased with himself, too – he had managed to find the man he was looking for and had talked with him about the timetable of our visit. First on the agenda was a dinner. We had been invited to go straight away to a meal with various farmers. The news was greeted with applause. We broke into small groups and went off to the nearby cottages.

I sat with Wojtek Gruda and two of my colleagues at a long, rough table in an overheated country kitchen, feeling very uneasy. The family of the hospitable farmer who had invited us clearly did not intend to eat with us. The wife and teenage daughter bustled about, serving us with piping-hot beetroot soup and potatoes seasoned with pork cracklings. The young children of the house gazed at us in bewilderment, while the farmer himself snored in an adjoining room.

Warmed by this substantial food we went back to the school. Again there was nothing to do as the community meeting had been arranged for the late afternoon. We had a couple of hours to fill so we decided to decorate the classrooms. We brought in from the van some posters we had been given to bring by the Party district committee and began to stick them on the walls. The posters called on all poor farmers to fight together in the class struggle against the kulaks*. The slogans were printed in big red capitals; the rough cartoons showed hideous overfed kulaks being trampled underfoot by handsome country lads dressed in shabby clothes. Soon the classrooms looked like a funfair. It looked ridiculous and I suggested we take some of the posters down and make our own – something more suitable. The team immediately voted in favour of this suggestion. Down came two or three posters and we set about making a more suitable one. I composed on the spot a lengthy poem about frendship between town and country people – how we knew so little about each other and should know more. One of my colleagues wrote a funny story in which a poor farmer tried to convince his reluctant wife to join a collective. Someone else drew a simple but nice cartoon and the new poster was stuck to the wall. Then it was time to go to the meeting.

The stuffy hall of the community social centre was already full when we arrived. Three members of the local council were sitting at a table facing the audience. Wojtek Gruda sat down next to them and the meeting began. Addressing the audience as 'neighbours' and calling us 'the town folks', the chairman announced that we had come to the village to talk about collectivisation. He appealed to his neighbours to speak their minds on the subject and to ask as many questions as they liked. A sudden burst of laughter came from the crowd as he finished, but otherwise the audience remained silent. Gruda stood up and began his speech.

* Kulaks – rich farmers.

He appealed to the farmers to speak up and tell us about their lives and worries, their daily hardships and any injustices they had suffered. He said that he had spent the first half of his life as a country boy and knew only too well what it was like to live in squalor and slave for the rich. However, everything had changed for the better for him in our young democratic country. Now he lived in comfort and dignity, enjoying freedom and social justice. 'You too could live like this,' he pleaded. 'All you have to do is to join forces against the exploiters, build a strong collective and share in the fruits of your labour.'

He spoke well, simply and sincerely, avoiding slogans. The audience, however, seemed unimpressed. When he stopped there was dead silence. The head of the council stared anxiously around, wondering what to do next. Then, suddenly, from the back of the crowd, came a shrill voice: a woman shrieked that her neighbour had beaten her teenage son for stealing apples from his tree. 'It's a lie,' she screamed. 'My son is an honest boy, he never steals. You people from the town,' she suddenly addressed Gruda, 'you, who speak of justice, do something about it.'

Before Wojtek could open his mouth, a burst of excited shouts broke out from the assembly, turning the silent crowd into an angrily buzzing beehive. Everyone suddenly had something to say – either in favour of or against the plaintiff and her son. The group broke into two warring camps. The men roared, the women screamed, the helpless chairman made desperate efforts to silence them but was completely ignored. At last, as the row turned into a fullscale fight, he walloped the table with both his fists and announced the end of the meeting. The uproar stopped for a moment and Gruda took his chance to speak for the last time. He said our team would now go back to the school and wait there in case any of the farmers would like to come and discuss the problems of collectivisation. Then twelve young people in green shirts and red ties beat a retreat from the newly raging battlefield.

We lit a fire in one of the freezing classrooms and sat round waiting. It was already dark, our faces lit only by firelight. We were tired and miserable. Some of the couples whispered and kissed in the darkness. Looking away, I could feel Gruda's longing gaze upon me. Two hours passed. Nobody turned up.

We set off for home late at night. There was no singing this time, people dozed off as soon as the van started. Half asleep, I thought about the wasted day. We had made fools of ourselves. I suddenly felt terribly sorry for myself, for my husband, and my child. Sunday was over – lost, away from my loved ones. A new week of hard work was about to begin.

Some time after the wretched expedition and partly as its result, my ZMP organisation honoured me with a permanent assignment: I was to be in charge of our internal 'newspaper' – a typed and hand-illustrated sheet, usually displayed on the walls of the entrance hall in the main building to be read by staff and visitors. At this time the Party was encouraging everybody – members and non-members alike – openly to express their criticisms of anything they thought wrong at work or in people's attitudes and behaviour, and also to criticise themselves publicly for their own shortcomings. The slogan of the day – 'Criticism and self-criticism are oxygen to the lungs of the Party' – was taken up by our organisation and activated in the columns of our 'wall paper'.

Using short, witty articles, sharp satirical poems and cartoons, we revelled in attacking bureaucrats, the snobs who looked up to the West, pompous stars of the prewar cinema, and the social climbers in the new regime. There were plenty of them around, if you looked closely. I loved this voluntary work and was happy to do it on top of my daily duties as editor of foreign films. Soon the 'wall paper' became extremely popular in the Studio, people could hardly wait to see new issues and came up with all sorts of ideas of their own. The people we criticised felt offended, sometimes hurt, and must have bitterly resented my role in the whole undertaking, but they seldom complained. The Party organisation was very pleased with our editorial team and encouraged our efforts. On one occasion I was awarded a prize 'for professional achievements and deep involvement in social activity'. And this was how Natalia, the head of Newsreels, turned up in my life.

As an executive of the Studio's Party organisation, she invited me to her editorial hut to congratulate me on my success. We had a friendly chat. She was an unusual woman, quick and clever, with a keen eye and a sharp tongue. Though very small and inconspicuous with her closely cropped, mousy hair and simple clothes, she inspired great respect and trust. When she said I should not distance myself from the Party I knew at once that I would become a member. Now or never. I told her I wanted to join.

A few days later I was invited to Natalia's office to be interviewed by the executive committee of the Party organisation. There were three or four people all together. They asked me many personal questions but uttered no slogans about the great task facing the country or the need to build socialism. I liked it better this way. I felt I could trust these people. They promised to discuss my application at a forthcoming Party meeting.

This meeting, which was to decide whether to accept me on a year's probation as a candidate for Party membership, took place in May. It was a beautiful day, full of sunshine and fragrant blossom. About thirty members gathered in the Studio's canteen that afternoon; I knew most of them, and they knew me. I felt at home. Natalia read out my application, a brief account of my life, and tabled a motion for my membership, adding some words of her own in support. Diana was the first to speak in my favour, referring to the time when she had been my immediate boss and giving a flattering description of my character. Several other members followed her, all speaking well of me. Some asked questions about my family life and studies, anxious to know whether I would be able to combine my new commitments with the ones I already had. Unabashed, I promised to try my best. As the discussion was coming to an end, a softly spoken, unassuming film director, Andrzej Munk, soon to become a leading light in the Polish cinema, raised his hand to ask about my Zionist past, which I had mentioned in my c.v. He wanted to know what had made me change my views so radically within the last three years. My answer to this question was my finest hour. Though usually shy of speaking in public, I felt elated. I told them all about my bitter experiences that, soon after the war, had made me want to leave Poland; about the crude Marxists, such as my first boss, who had made me hate the very name of the Party; about the true Marxism I had come to know while studying; and about my husband who had finally helped me to believe in socialism and trust the Party. My speech was greeted with a storm of applause. Everyone clapped, including Andrzej Munk. The motion was passed unanimously and I was accepted as a candidate for Party membership on one year's probation.

My departure was like a beautiful dream. A little crowd of Party comrades saw me off at the Studio gate, under trees in full blossom. The personnel manager, Wojtek Gruda, offered me a huge bunch of fragrant lilac. I was hugged, kissed and showered with congratulations. I was happy.

So now I was a communist. A real one. Not a communist by moral instinct or creed or circumstantial compromise: a card-carrying member of the Party. My sense of moral instinct and belief suddenly became unimportant. I agreed to accept the Party's decisions on matters right and wrong and to leave it to the Party to choose which articles of faith to preach and which not to bother about. In exchange for my freedom of choice, the Party gave me the security of being always in the right and having no doubts. At least that is what it said in the small print of the unwritten contract I had signed on that happy day. But I never read the small print.

Could I have? Some people did. And it was written all around me, in big capital letters. I could have read it in the manic glee of my first boss's eyes, on the face of the defenceless Jacqueline, in the sly grin of Barski, in the self-righteous posturing of red dignitaries, in the play-acting of their wives, in the sullen silence of the peasants. But I didn't. Or perhaps I did – only I refused to understand the meaning of what I read.

The Party never asked to be judged by the morality of its actions. Its kingdom was not of this world. It beckoned to the future. And the future was all bliss – without hatred or prejudice, race or nation. Was this not the world I had dreamed of ever since my life behind the ghetto walls? Was it not the only world in which, once and for all, my dream of belonging would come true?

Did I have any such thoughts on that sunny day? I have no idea. I can't remember what questions I asked myself. Perhaps I did not ask any. Perhaps I simply did not think about how I had arrived where I now found myself – or what my route had been. Maybe there were no questions to ask. Maybe it all seemed natural to me, normal, logical, ordinary, expectable.

I do not remember scaling any heights of mental debate or leaping any moral chasms in my mind. My road was made of small steps: a record of a friendly chat; a Sunday in a village; a joke in the wall paper ... None of these seemed so important, just natural and right. There were no points of no return, no moments of momentous decision. Things just happened to me; I moved more or less effortlessly where the tide carried me.

Though there was no point of no return, and I could perhaps have turned back at any point, the Party saw to it that my decision seemed irreversible. This was its power, its craft. My children, my grandchildren beware. There is no fair play in the game of power, no small steps, no meeting halfway with a chance of return. Beware of those who promise you to bear responsibility for your deeds. What they want is your compliance. The responsibility will remain your own. Ignorance is no excuse for complicity. Do not let the powerful catch hold of your finger: they take your whole arm. And you will not even notice when they engulf the rest of you.

Something was going wrong with the Six Year Economic Plan. Despite all the promises, the standards of living dropped and inflation was rising. There were immediate repercussions in our daily life: shortages in basic articles, ever longer queues in the shops, salaries running out before the end of the month, wages before the end of the week. It looked as though the whole grandiose plan to enrich the nation had totally misfired.

In June 1951 the government, strongly backed by the Party, launched a National Development Loan of 1200 million zloties.

All citizens were urged to contribute. Party activists were summoned and told to explain to the reluctant how important the loan was for the future of the country. For the first time I was acknowledged as a Party activist and told to work with comrade Gruda. We spent three long days preaching on behalf of the National Development Loan to small-time shopkeepers, doctors and dentists, even to some nuns in a little convent. The days were bright and warm. Wandering from place to place, entering the unfamiliar homes and private lives of strangers, which at first felt like trespassing, soon became a romantic adventure. Wojtek was a handsome, eloquent man; I was good-looking, too, and a little shy. People, even those who at first greeted us with barely concealed hostility, eventually came to like us and signed the appeal, making their small contributions. The most generous were the nuns. They asked us to share their simple meal and we had a friendly talk with them at the table. I felt we had done an excellent job, and this was soon confirmed by our Party superiors. I was pleased with myself, even though while I was away Lena fell ill. Someone else was taking good care of my sick child, so I could feel free to sacrifice myself for the well-being of my country. My conscience was clear.

There were no clouds in the blue sky that hot summer of 1951, no distant rumbles threatened my happy life. Everything went well: I passed my final exams and got my BA degree; Lena went to the countryside with Pani Waczkowska; my favourite major, sun-tanned and strikingly handsome, enjoyed life as much as myself. I loved my work and hoped to get an even better job – a film director wanted me as his assistant. This was planned for the coming autumn. First I was to take my annual summer leave and have a rest.

One of us had to stay in Warsaw to go and see Lena from time to time, so Konrad took holidays alone. When he returned at the end of August, I was getting ready to leave for Zakopane, where a room had been booked for me in a rest-house. At the very last moment, however, I received an urgent piece of work which I had to deal with before I left.

A full-length documentary film from the Soviet Union had just arrived at the Studio. It had been made to celebrate the forthcoming second anniversary of the German Democratic Republic. It showed the achievements of the young republic and the celebrations for the first anniversary ten months earlier in which all the leaders of the Eastern countries and heads of the communist parties had taken part. The film had already been given Polish subtitles by the Russians, but they were not good enough and needed replacing with more Polish-sounding ones. It was me who had to do it and do it fast.

This was a nuisance. The film included many long, dry, political speeches. I had to check against the official Polish translations which had appeared in the press about a year earlier. This involved long hours of searching in the archives. It took me several days to find everything I needed, to edit the rest and to compile a complete list of all the corrections needed. I hastily dictated this endlessly long list to the typist, read it over and signed it in a great hurry. I then had it signed by the chief editor and the head of the Studio, before leaving on holiday.

The following night I found myself on a train speeding towards Zakopane to my well-deserved rest. As an officer's wife I enjoyed the privilege of staying in a military rest-house even when my husband was not with me. Some of Konrad's colleagues and their wives were there to keep me company. The weather was brilliant, the high Tatra mountains stood out sharply against the cloudless sky – austere and seemingly impenetrable but just asking to be climbed. Every day, with a small group of fellow-climbers, I went off on long excursions into the heart of the mountains, sometimes spending a night or two in an alpine shelter or simply in a barn full of hay.

One evening at sunset, just down from the peak of Giewont, deadly tired and sore but radiant, I was stopped in the entrance hall of the rest-house by the receptionist: there was a telegram waiting for me. It said simply, 'Return at once' and was signed by Diana.

After a sleepless night of fruitless speculations, I embarked on my trip home and arrived back late the following night. Konrad, who knew nothing about the telegram, was taken by surprise. He was very alarmed. We spent long hours together trying to guess the reason for this sudden summons.

When I arrived at the Studio in the morning I found myself in a Kafkaesque world of eerie silence. My fellow editors knew that something strange had been brewing up around me but they had no idea what it was about. Their eyes were sympathetic but they said nothing. My immediate boss, the chief editor, was absent. I was told that she had suddenly resigned three days before. I reported to Diana but her secretary said she was too busy to see me now. The door of the director's office stood ajar: he was out, his desk was neatly cleared. Natalia, to whom I finally turned, hoping that she, as a Party executive, would tell me what was going on, knew no more than anyone else – or perhaps did not want to say what she knew. I returned to my hut and sat idle – not knowing what to do next. Then the telephone rang. The personnel manager, Wojtek Gruda, had a message for me: I must go at once to the headquarters in Pulawska Street and see someone – no name or official rank was given – in room number thirteen.

Room number thirteen turned out to be a strangely hidden place, tucked away amongst storerooms and brush-cupboards in a rear extension of the high building where I had worked at the beginning of my film career. I had never noticed it before. Its door was padded with some thick, soft stuff and was hardly visible in the dark corridor. It was impossible to knock on this soft surface, so I entered without knocking. It was a very small, dark room, almost empty except for a desk, two chairs and a conventional print of the profiles of Marx, Engels, Lenin and Stalin, glued to the wall. A stranger, a dreary man with a grey face and blank eyes sat at the desk reading a newspaper. Addressing me as 'citizen' he told me to sit down on the second chair. He produced a notebook from his pocket and, scanning its contents, started to check all my personal details, as if to make sure I was indeed the person he wanted to see. Satisfied on this point, he handed me an untidy typescript and ordered me to take a close look at it. It was the list of subtitles for the Russian film about East Germany. 'Do you know this typescript, citizen?' he asked icily. Yes, indeed,

I knew it, I had worked damn hard on it just before my holiday, I told him. 'Do you recognise this signature?' he enquired, showing me the last page of the typescript and pointing with his filthy fingernail at the two words scribbled at the foot. It was my signature, of course, and I confirmed this. 'So you don't deny, citizen, that you wrote this text,' he stated rather than asked. Of course I did not. With a sparkle of something that could have been a triumphant grin, he rapidly started turning over the pages and stopped somewhere in the middle. I saw here a paragraph circled in red ink and a huge, red exclamation mark popping out in the margin. He let me read in silence.

It was a fragment of Stalin's official speech in which he congratulated the German president, Wilhelm Pieck, on the achievements of the young democratic republic. It read: 'Your nation have chosen a shameful way . . .' I felt my blood freeze: a disastrous mistake had somehow crept into my typescript. It should have read 'glorious way' – this was what was written in the official translation of Stalin's speech and what I had dictated to the typist. In a flash I understood: I was suspected of political sabotage. I must have turned very pale, as my interrogator, who had been keeping a sharp eye on me all the time, suddenly offered to bring me a glass of water. Then, in an oddly soft way, he asked me to explain why had I put such an incredible word into the mouth of comrade Stalin.

Yes, I had already guessed and could explain what had happened. The Polish words for 'glorious' and 'shameful' – *'chwalebny'* and *'haniebny'* – cannot possibly be confused if they are written down; but they sound quite alike when spoken. So, the typist must have got it wrong when I dictated the sentence. I told the man with the blank eyes what I thought and admitted that I had read the typescript in great haste before signing it. He stared at me blankly. I could not tell whether he believed me or not. Anyway, he changed his tune and showered me with questions about the typist. Who was she? Her name, surname and age, please. How long had I known her? What did she do in her spare time? (How on earth could I know this?) Any boyfriends, girl-friends, contacts with the West? Had she ever expressed her political views? Exasperated, I tried to stop his questions; I swore that Basia, the typist, was a silly girl with no political views whatever, and very dull too; if she had been a little brighter, she would never have typed the word 'shameful' in Stalin's congratulation speech. The man was taking hasty notes. The interrogation was over. He told me to go straight home and to wait there until further notice.

On the following day I was summoned to see Diana. Usually calm and reserved, she looked distressed. Her handsome face bore signs of fatigue or maybe sleepless nights. In a strangely stumbling way she told me that I had been dismissed from my post in the Studio and should not return to work. Without looking at me she said my mistake was very serious and I would have to be severely punished. On the other hand, she stressed, it was clear that it was a mistake not a deliberate piece of mischief, and this meant that the film authorities would be able to offer me another job outside the Studio – a less responsible job, though, and much lower paid. I accepted the verdict in silence.

I had to stay at the Studio till the afternoon, since an extraordinary Party meeting had been called to investigate my case. I was supposed to make a self-criticising speech and might well be expelled from the Party.

In the canteen that had seen my triumph five months earlier, the same people gathered again. This time no one smiled at me. There was little discussion, either: the comrades sat in dismal silence. Trembling, I stood up and made a short speech. I said I was terribly ashamed of having been so absent-minded and promised that, once bitten twice shy, I would be deadly careful with Stalin's words, if by chance I ever had cause to deal with them again. Nobody applauded when I finished, but no motion for my expulsion was proposed. People left in silence. Many of those who once had kissed and hugged me in the same canteen, now passed me by like strangers. Yet, some did stop and kiss me goodbye. Some had tears in their eyes. The personnel manager, Wojtek Gruda, his eyes turned away, his face stony, secretly squeezed my hand while passing.

The penalty was hard to bear and for a while robbed me of all joy in life. I was back in the headquarters at Puławska Street, grinding away as a grade eight reader of projects for short educational films. The film studio was far away in Łódź. They sent their projects for official approval and I was one of the team who had to examine them. They were interesting projects and the educational films did a good job – for school children and cinema audiences alike. But most of the subjects I knew little about and was not interested in. As I sat there reading for hours about the structure of the hind legs of the burying beetle or about how a conveyor belt moves, I would find myself constantly dropping asleep. I felt as though I was gradually withering away. My colleagues were bored to death, too. Like myself, they all seemed to have been sent to serve a sentence. Our immediate boss was a stupid woman who knew nothing about the cinema. The obvious ignorance of my boss was for me the worst punishment.

In fact, I should have been grateful to Providence for having saved me from a far more sinister fate. How bad things could have been I only learned a few days after leaving the Documentary Studio when Wojtek Gruda paid me an unexpected visit. In a strange way, this gentle, trustworthy man seemed to be always in the know about all sorts of things that were supposed to be secret; stranger still, he was quite happy to tell me what he knew or guessed.

He called on me in my new office and suggested we went out together for a short chat. There was, he said, an empty office on the premises where we could talk in private. Intrigued, I followed him to the extension at the back of the main building and suddenly found myself in the same room where, several days earlier, I had been interrogated by the dreary stranger. Gruda laughed when I told him this. He was really a dear friend. I could tell that his feelings for myself were a little more than friendly. We sat down on the two chairs facing each other and I heard the full story of my wretched typescript.

When I had left for my holidays the list of subtitles was sent to the Film Export and Import Office to be signed there by three high-ranking officials, who, in turn, passed it on to their Russian counterparts for their approval. The Russians were the first to spot the fatal mistake, and suspecting an act of political sabotage, raised an alarm. The chairman of the Polish Film was woken in the middle of the night and summoned to U.B.* The following day, the three high-ranking officials in the import office were sacked on the spot, as were the head and the chief editor of the Documentary Studio. Yet it was I who was the main suspect and for a while it seemed I might be arrested and put on trial for political sabotage. 'Imagine where you would be by now,' Gruda laughed, 'if it hadn't been for Diana.' It was Diana, he said, who had saved me, by vouching for my innocence. Her word was accepted and the sentence was reduced to 'guilty of an unforgivable oversight'. The U.B.'s suspicion then fell on the typist Basia. But, Gruda stressed, she had been cleared too and was not even fired from work.

Shattered, I sat in silence. Only now did I realise how grave my predicament had been. Gruda stroked my hair and said I shouldn't think about it, everybody knew I was an honest, hardworking person and a devoted member of the Party. Not like some of my new colleagues, he sighed, who had an unsavoury political record and should never have been trusted. Surprised, I asked who he meant. The woman who worked next to me, he said, a certain Beata. During the German occupation she was involved in the underground movement and had belonged to the AK, the Home Army, which – as we all knew – was strongly nationalistic, and though fighting against the Nazis had regarded the Soviet Union as another enemy of Poland. Beata had been an AK officer and taken an active part in the Warsaw uprising. Soon after the war she was arrested by the new Polish authorities and was only released after serving a sentence. Besides, she was a devoted Catholic and a keen church-goer. People of her kind, Gruda repeated, could not be trusted: they tended to maintain suspicious contacts with the West and could bring harm to our cause.

I did not like what he said. Beata was the only one of my new

* The Secret Police

colleagues who I had liked at first sight. She was bright and capable but at the same time modest, even humble. She looked harassed, wore shabby clothes and seemed half-starved. In her early thirties and unmarried, she supported her old mother, earning less than I did even though I earned very little. I could swear she had nothing to do with imperialism or any political activity. I told Gruda what I thought, but he laughed again and said I might change my opinion if I made friends with Beata and learnt more about her private life. 'Next time I come to see you,' he said, warmly squeezing my hand, 'you'll be telling me I was quite right.' We parted cordially but I was left with an unpleasant feeling that Wojtek wanted to see me again for reasons other than just being attracted to me. However, it was disgraceful to think like that about a good friend, so I dismissed the thought at once.

On Thursdays I make pots. The heavy lump of cool, moist clay wedged and turned, squeezed and slapped, cut into halves then smartly brought back together by banging against the hard, rough surface of the concrete bench, starts yielding to my impatient fingers. One more cut, one more bang and soft, smooth, consenting, it's ready to be shaped.

Sitting at a long table in the studio, my hands busy, my mind full, I listen absent-mindedly to the chatter of my fellow-potters. They speak about the miners' strike, the danger of Aids, about a farmer who tried to kill his wife. I don't hear the full story, my thoughts are with the clay. I tear it in pieces, I roll little coils, I build up the sides of my simple pot. Now the pot is finished, still crude and dull but firm. Later, it will come out of the kiln as pale as a raw loaf of bread, begging for a stroke of paint, a splash of glaze. And when it comes out of the fire for the second time, I'll take it home and put it on the window-sill to regale my eyes with its roundness, its tanned crust parched like sun-burst soil.

Week after week, month after month over the last few years, I've been making these jugs and bowls, mugs and teapots. Some are wobbly, some are warped but I like them all since I've made them with my own ten fingers.

Those ten fingers of mine were said to be good for nothing when I was a child. I believed this and never thought twice about it for over fifty years: a lousy cook, a wretched housewife who wouldn't iron her husband's shirt or darn her children's socks.

The most my fingers could do was type. Only when I retired and could at last do whatever I wanted, did I make up my mind to challenge my fingers. The first little vase, doomed to failure, it seemed, turned out to be a small success. You should never believe you're good for nothing until you've tried.

A pot is a thing of substance. You can handle it, you can lift it, you can drink from it or use it for flowers. A pot is a thing that did not exist before you produced it; it is a brand-new object brought into being by yourself. Friends are pleased to be given pots, strangers sometimes buy them. Making pots can do harm to nobody. One can't ever be blamed for making pots.

I think I've wasted a good deal of my life toiling at things that were evasive, ambiguous, maybe harmful sometimes – and producing nothing. My next film career which took many long years and led from one success to another finally left me empty-handed: when the time came to say goodbye, nothing was left behind me.

*

This long career began as the result of a tragic accident. In the winter of 1951–2 the government's ruthless economic policy had further disastrous consequences. The collectivisation of farming forced upon farmers usually against their will reduced from month to month the supply of food in the shops. Rationing was introduced. Meat became a rarity and only those with an income well above the average could afford to eat it often. They bought it at soaring prices on the black market. This meat, produced, stored and delivered illegally, sometimes in totally unsanitary conditions, caused incidents of serious food poisoning. In February 1952, appalling news shattered the daily routine of our office: an editor in the Script Bureau, a successful young woman, was desperately ill from a particularly lethal form of food poisoning. When the doctors were fighting for Alicja's life, Marta, the chief editor in the Script Bureau, found herself without her only assistant. This was at a time when the production of full-length Polish feature films had been gathering momentum and the

Bureau was inundated with projects, novels, short stories and film scripts that needed to be read and accepted or rejected. Marta had a team of clerical and administrative staff, but no one to replace Alicja. She turned to me. A homely, unassertive, rather plain woman in her thirties, she came to my office where I was poring over a project on different methods of bricklaying, and asked me whether as a favour I could read a few scripts in my spare time. She said she had heard a lot about me from her close friend and flat-mate, Natalia, the head of the Newsreel. Marta had brought two bulky typescripts with her and showed them to me apologetically – it was a lot of reading compared with the slim scripts for educational films. If I could read them, she said, she would want me to write reports and preferably also make recommendations. Flattered and excited, I didn't hesitate for a moment. I said I could start reading that very night if it was urgent. Yes, it was urgent, Marta said, the authors were pressing for decisions, the directors were impatient to start on new films, the studio in Łódź was ready and waiting for work. Unfortunately, she explained, there was no money involved, she could not pay me for my work, she was only asking me as a favour. I said that was all right. I wasn't worried about the money, just wanted to read the scripts – I longed for a glimpse into the magic world of screened fiction. At the same time, I was a little nervous: would I be as good as Alicja? I had never read her reports, but I had always assumed that her judgement must be superb. She looked so competent – so resolute and self-reliant – everything I lacked myself. I told Marta honestly what I thought but she didn't seem worried. 'Let's try,' she said. 'There's nothing to lose.'

Two days later I brought Marta my reports and I could see straight away that she liked what I had written. They were both very critical, they both recommended rejection, but each for totally different reasons. One of the scripts I reported on was a skilfully written comedy of errors, with a hackneyed plot and unconvincing characters, very much in the tradition of prewar Polish routine comedies. The other was about a country youth who found his happiness in the town by becoming an exemplary factory worker and an ardent Party activist. This script lacked any literary values, it sinned against all the rules of dramatic plot, was long-winded and positively dull. When Marta finished reading my reports, she sighed and said she trusted my opinion and would not even bother to read the scripts herself. She gave me more to work on in my spare time: Alicja was still in hospital and was showing no signs of improvement.

Some time later Alicja died, in her prime. The following day the job of script editor was offered to me.

So, there I was, back in my element again. My sin had obviously been expiated and forgiven, my salary was handsomely raised, my self-confidence restored. Once again I immersed myself in work with all my heart and soul. My new surroundings had none of the freedom I had enjoyed so much in the Documentary Studio, but the work was exciting. Every project and script I read developed in my mind into a full-scale film. I was free to write whatever I liked about these 'films', to investigate them in detail and make my own suggestions on improvement. Marta and the Programme director, and their superiors, read my reports carefully: it helped them to form their own opinions, to discuss the scripts with the authors, and finally to reach a decision. No film could go into production without its script being finally approved by the top people in the industry.

All material submitted was judged in accordance with the principles of socialist realism – or soc-realism as we called it. Films like literature and other works of art had to play a part in the struggle for socialism. By the time I became a script editor, this theory, conceived and implemented in the Soviet Union long before, had already resulted in a score of second-rate Polish films. As a rule, they showed blameless heroes fighting repulsive villains. They painted a colourful picture of our society that had very little to do with the drabness of real life. They could hardly be considered works of art. Yet the people responsible for the development of the new Polish cinema still strained their minds – if not always their hearts – to follow the commandments of soc-realism. Working in the Script Bureau on the lowest rung of the ideological ladder, I became one of them. I didn't yet realise in 1952 that we, the editors, were working more or less as censors.

We did our work with a lot of good will and with deep conviction. We often strongly disapproved of decisions made by the professional censors who looked at films as though they were newspaper editorials and cut them as they wished, refusing to accept that they were also works of art. Yet, to some extent, we were players in the same game. The spirit of censorship reached far and deep. Even the authors had by then absorbed this spirit and very few of them wrote anything that might upset the censors.

I liked my work and wanted to be a really good editor. I felt I had a lot more to learn about script writing, about the language of film and the process of film-making. There were no schools for script writers or editors; the prestigious Film Academy in Łódź catered only for film directors and cameramen. So I had to learn mainly by reading and gaining experience at work. Marta was only too keen to help. She was relatively new in the field herself, and had only got where she was through hard learning. Staff visiting from the Łódź Film Academy gave lectures on the history and theory of film, and these we both attended. But this was not enough. I wanted to know everything about the whole process of film-making – from the germ of an idea in the head of a writer or director, to the finished picture on the screen. So, with Marta's blessing, I travelled to Łódź quite often to visit the studio and silently watched a scene being shot, a new setting being arranged, the actors being instructed on how to deliver their lines. Or if someone was filming in the streets of Warsaw I would rush out from our office in the middle of the day to see scenes being shot on location. Whenever a new film was finished it was sent from Łódź to the headquarters to be viewed for the first time by Very Important Persons. I was allowed to attend these exclusive showings and, sitting in the familiar darkness of the little projection room on the fifth floor, I would compare the picure on the screen with the images I had conjured up when reading the script. It was fascinating, and very instructive too.

At this stage of my editorial career I had little to do with the scriptwriters, film directors or producers themselves – they would pass through my office on their way to see Marta, sometimes stopping to exchange a few polite words, sometimes not. The other people in my office worked on contracts or did clerical work, and were far less privileged than I: they never attended the exclusive shows or went out on location. Nor were they entitled to the monthly rations of real coffee which I received and which at the time was strictly reserved for artists and writers. So I was singled out in my new surroundings and hovered, as it were, between the peak and foot of Mount Olympus. I felt quite lonely. One person I would gladly have kept in touch with was Beata in the educational department, but she disappeared soon after I moved to the Script Bureau. One day she left and I heard she had been made a junior clerk in a film warehouse. Nobody knew why, but some thought it was due to her political views. With her nationalism and bigotry, they said, she could hardly expect to stay long as an editor in the educational department. Gruda's words now sounded more like a sinister warning than idle gossip. I wondered how Beata's beliefs could possibly have damaged the films on burying beetles or conveyor belts, but somehow I never thought of asking my Party organisation this question.

Wojtek Gruda was still a good friend. He had left the Documentary Studio and now worked in the headquarters too. He never said what kind of work he did and dismissed any questions about this with a joke. We always met at our Party meetings and sat whispering together in the crowded room. This helped to pass the long hours of dreadful boredom. I attended these meetings regularly but never felt deeply involved. The problems discussed were usually very trivial. Most of the members were departmental directors and managers and carried on long and heated arguments on issues thought up mainly to sustain their own prestige. Some junior clerks came too but they always kept quiet. The working class was represented by an elderly driver who claimed he had taken part in the Russian Revolution, and by a senile lift-man who would suddenly raise his hand and loudly berate the comrades for not going to church. Some caretakers and canteen attendants would fall asleep immediately the meeting began, only waking up at the end when the assembly burst into the

Internationale. In May, a year after I had been accepted as a Party candidate, this peculiar organisation voted in favour of my permanent membership. This time I did not feel overjoyed.

At first I had no special Party assignments or functions, and since I had finished my studies I was able to spend more time with my family. Lena was now three years old and had grown into a cheerful, talkative child. She was very pretty, too, but very poorly dressed. Children's clothes available in the shops were usually rough, in nondescript colours. It was hard to find the right size of anything you needed. So, everything Lena wore was dark-brown or navy-blue, too long or too short. I felt very embarrassed whenever a friend remarked that such a pretty little girl with such beautiful dark wavy hair and eyes like a pair of blue stars deserved something better. Nobody in the household could alter Lena's clothes or make a proper dress for her. Pani Waczkowska was far too busy, Zofia, whose health was fast deteriorating, returned from work exhausted and went straight to bed. I was convinced I was hopeless at sewing, so I never even tried. Instead, I spent my spare time with Lena reading her fairy tales or telling her stories I made up myself. Perhaps this somewhat lopsided kind of motherly care was the reason why my poor little Cinderella has later become a highly intellectual woman who can never resist buying the most expensive clothes. Anyway, we were both very happy as I read and she listened, nestling lovingly against me.

At this time Konrad decided to continue his studies and joined a part-time M.A. course in philosophy and social sciences. He spent his evenings poring over books and manuscripts again. His work in the military unit now seemed much less exciting than before. The respectable old colonel was gone and had been replaced by someone else whom Konrad neither liked nor respected. Rumours were circulating that the colonel had been transferred to a less responsible post because he was Jewish. Some claimed he had applied for this transfer himself, being convinced that no one trusted him because he was a Jew. All this was hard to believe. The idea that anti-Semitism could take over again in a society that was striving to build socialism was unthinkable, totally incompatible with what the government, the Party and we ourselves stood for. Yet, events in the Soviet Union seemed to confirm the unbelievable. In December 1952, Stalin ordered the arrest of a group of Kremlin doctors, most of whom were Jews, on a charge of murdering some Politburo members and conspiring to murder others. This was a signal for an anti-Semitic purge which swept the Soviet Union. Though daily worried by what we read between the lines and by the anxious whispers of some Jewish friends, we still tried to deny the truth of the obvious. Perhaps there was a higher reason behind the pending trial? Perhaps there really had been some plot after all? Anyway, in our country things like that couldn't happen. We were free to live in peace and enjoy the high winter season for dancing parties.

Once in January 1953 Konrad and I spent an exhilarating night at a showy officers' ball in the barracks. With Adam and a dozen other friendly officers we drank, sang and danced till the morning. Twenty-four hours later, Konrad was summoned to his new boss and dismissed from the army on the spot.

This was a terrible shock, a bolt from the blue. It knocked Konrad off his feet and for a while dimmed his powers of judgement. The reason given for this sudden dismissal was that his father had maintained some suspicious contacts with the West: he had, they said, been a regular visitor to the Israeli embassy. In agony, Konrad went straight to his father. The old man did not deny it: he had been to the Israeli embassy twice to ask their advice about emigration. In a state of frantic despair, Konrad accused him of being secretive and plotting behind his back.

Tense silence fell upon our happy home, even Lena stopped laughing. Every morning I left Konrad staring blankly at his books, and on my return in the evening would find him in the same position. A week passed before he pulled himself together and went to the university. When on the same day I came back from work, I found his parents' room deserted: they had left, taking with them most of their belongings. They had left no word and only the nanny knew their new address. I thought Konrad would go straight after his parents and beg them to come back. But he grew obstinate, shrank into himself and did absolutely nothing. Nevertheless, I knew how much suffering this new blow caused him.

All of a sudden we found ourselves in an empty world. No friends called to cheer us up, not even Adam. The officers with whom we had spent the hilarious night a few days before crossed the street to avoid meeting us face to face. Neighbours on the staircase turned their eyes away. Only my mother and Sophie called from time to time, puzzled, worried and helpless.

Konrad's university seminars and my daily work were now our only links with the outside world. Konrad had on his dismissal been offered a post in a civilian ministry, but he refused to accept it. He decided, instead, to concentrate on his studies, and buried himself in work, spending all days and nights on it. He was no longer the same person. The radiant, zestful boy became a weary man. His grudge against his father was turning into deep sorrow and bitter anxiety about his parents' fate.

Knowing this and feeling extremely sorry for my in-laws too, I once, without Konrad's knowledge, took Lena and went to see them. They were living in the Old Town, in a single room at the back of the big restaurant run by Zofia. They were surprised, overjoyed and very grateful to me for having brought them their beloved granddaughter. Zofia's health had deteriorated again and she could hardly walk, her legs swollen and threatened with gangrene. But she still worked as usual, her ambition and strong will keeping her up and about. I shyly suggested they come back and live with us again, but they were proud people and flatly refused: they were fine on their own, they said. Konrad pretended not to listen when I later told him about this visit.

Very soon, any hope of my parents-in-law returning home became impossible. Without warning, a junior officer and his wife moved into our empty room. Some unfamiliar towels and toothbrushes appeared in our little bathroom, a dozen alien pans and plates in the kitchen. We were no longer alone.

My salary was now our only income. Though relatively high, it was far from enough to support the four of us: Lena had to be sent to nursery school and Pani Waczkowska dismissed – we could no longer afford her wages and keep. It was a heartbreaking experience for her and for us, but most of all for Lena. She loved her nanny dearly and when taken to the nursery for the first time, she refused to stay there, hoping that we might change our minds and bring her nanny back. But we could not do that.

Like many other things introduced after the war, nursery schools were a real blessing to working women. They were free and children of working mothers could be left there eight hours a day. The children were usually well fed and cared for. Despite her initial rebellion, Lena quickly got used to her new way of life and being sociable and confident by nature began to enjoy other children's company. I would drop her off each morning on my way to work and pick her up on my way home. Lena's problem was thus solved and this helped us greatly in making ends meet. Canteen meals were cheap so Konrad and I ate there at midday – I at work, he at the university. Konrad dyed two of his military uniforms civilian colours, and this solved more or less the problem of his clothes. Dressed in horrid brown, he still looked very attractive. Little by little we came to terms with our new circumstances and deep in my heart I rejoiced that Konrad was no longer in the army: I had never really liked his military service. After recovering from the initial shock, he learnt to appreciate his freedom. The world of knowledge now stood open to him – something he had longed for all his life.

Although all our uniformed friends had turned their backs on us, our home did not stay empty for long. New acquaintances soon began to pour in. Most of Konrad's colleagues at the University were four or five years younger than him. They had been born too late to take part in the war and had therefore never wasted their time slaving in the army. Most of them were very clever men and women, deeply committed to their studies and to the great changes that were taking place in the country. Many were already married and very wrapped up in their young families. At first some of them felt apprehensive in our company, though they later became close friends. Some didn't quite trust Konrad for having served in the communist army; others, on the contrary, were suspicious about his sudden dismissal. Some time passed before they got to know him well enough to judge him by his own standards.

Many years later, in England, we had to start from scratch again, strangers among strangers in our new country. We had to prove once more what we thought we had proved to the full in the past. To our new companions we were closed books arousing vague, undefined suspicions for the simple reason that they did not know us. How deep these suspicions went we only realised soon after we settled in Leeds when a new friend invited us to dinner. Charles was a university lecturer, very bright and gentle, young enough to be our son. He did his best to make the new professor and his wife feel at ease and had chosen a cosy little restaurant where we could talk intimately. We had an excellent meal together and drank very good wine. The conversation flowed smoothly without strain. Even I, usually shy with strangers and painfully aware of my hesitant English, joined in happily. I could feel a warm, friendly bond growing between us and Charles.

Then, suddenly, late on in the dinner, Charles raised his innocent eyes over his profiteroles and, staring anxiously into Konrad's eyes, fired this horrifying question: 'Is it true what they say,' he asked, his handsome, gentle face beaming with excitement, 'that you were a KGB agent?' The restaurant suddenly lost its charm. A large piece of pineapple stuck in my constricted throat. Konrad sat, ghostly pale, as though on the verge of heart failure. But he quickly pulled himself together. 'No,' he said, 'it's an utter lie.' Charles at once realised that he had made a *faux pas* and, feeling desperately sorry, began to explain what he had actually heard. What people had been talking about was, in fact, Konrad's communist past. Konrad has never denied his past political commitments or his life-long belief in socialism. Nor have I. We told Charles that we had both once belonged to the communist party. But this was nothing to do with working for the KGB or its Polish counterpart. Could he see the difference? He seemed a little confused. And so probably was everyone else with whom we were now living. There was no way of proving that we were telling the truth. We could only provide the evidence of our lives. And it would take years, at the least.

When, in March 1953, a couple of months after Konrad's discharge, Stalin died, no loud cheers or sighs of relief were heard in Poland. In common with many people around the world, our mourning was sincere. A great man was gone, a leader whose iron fist had crushed the Fascist ogre, who for years had stood alone against Nazi power and who now stood between us and a new war. We had lived for so many years in his shadow that it was difficult to see how life could go on without him. The fact that his death opened the way to momentous change was not something we could then see. At the start, nothing changed in our daily life or, for that matter, in the country as a whole. The world only seemed somewhat less safe.

At that time I was lecturer for the Party, a very responsible function. Once a week, on Monday morning, I had to give talks on the Russian Revolution and its aftermath to a group of comrades. There were many such courses at the film headquarters, as well as everywhere else in the country. The audience was usually chosen according to educational level. Since I was only a beginner in the field of political preaching, I was allocated a group of the lowest level: the kitchen staff, the door-keepers, the drivers. I hated this work but there was no way I could refuse. So I had to spend every Sunday preparing my talk and then pass a sleepless night dreading the morning. I was terribly shy as a lecturer and I had little interest in the topics I was supposed to discuss.

My audience usually sat dumb and silent during our sessions, half-dreaming of Sunday or thinking about the work that lay ahead and barely listening to my words. I put my heart and soul into making the story clear and exciting but I never felt it really went home. I would talk and talk for a solid hour but seldom got any response.

When Stalin died, the Central Committee of the Party instructed its lecturers to talk about his merits and fine deeds. I was just faltering out the recommended lines one Monday morning when I was suddenly interrupted. The old driver who claimed to have witnessed the Great October Revolution leapt up and said that all this was utter rubbish. Stalin, he said, was never loved in the old days; he was known as a wild, cruel man; people feared him, great Lenin positively hated him.

This speaking of the unspeakable came as a bombshell. It was my duty to respond at once, to find the strongest words I could to prove the old man wrong. But I was speechless. He must be mad. I guiltily made up my mind to turn a deaf ear to what he had said and to forget it if I could. But I was frightened that one of the audience might denounce the driver and also myself. In fact this never happened. Maybe because none of my students cared a damn about anything that was ever said during our Monday sessions. Soon this ordeal of lecturing, which had lasted several months, came to an end anyway when I was elected to the executive committee of our party organisation.

Since Konrad no longer served in the army, we were ordered at the beginning of the following autumn to leave our flat – another major needed it for his family. No one, however wicked politically or otherwise, could be left homeless in Poland, so the army moved us to another flat in a block of apartments inside some fenced military grounds guarded by sentries. It was a gloomy place and the flat was horrible: two dark little north-facing rooms looking out onto tall trees; a filthy kitchenette; a bathroom fit for a dwarf, always cold and with no hot water. We had to get rid of most of our furniture – there was simply no room for it. We put Lena's cot and all her belongings in one of the rooms, in the other our couch and a kitchen table for Konrad to write his M.A. thesis on. There was little space left to entertain our friends whose number had steadily grown. They had to obtain special entry permits every time they came to see us. A wretched time began.

Right at the start Lena caught a bad cold in the freezing bathroom and from then on spent more time in bed than in the nursery. I had to stay at home with her and missed a lot of work. Nobody held this against me and my salary was paid in full every month, but I couldn't bear getting behind. In the end a very old woman who lived nearby agreed to look after Lena whenever she was too poorly to go to nursery. It didn't cost much but we were so hard up it still made a difference. I remember days when there was nothing to eat in the evening. Sometimes because of lack of money, sometimes because the queues in the shops were so long; sometimes because there was simply no food to be bought. Konrad did everything he could to help, but he was studying full time now and his heart was set on completing his degree as soon as possible.

Despite all the hardships of this gloomy time, we were never really unhappy and only rarely grumbled. Other people around us had far greater cause to do so. One whose plight was infinitely worse than ours was my new colleague, Marek. He had been made second editor in the Script Bureau, to help cope with the steadily growing volume of work. A thin, pale, exhausted-looking man in his early thirties, Marek had an ailing wife and two young children who lived away in a provincial town. He was studying at the Academy in Łódź to become a film director. Since he also had to support his family, he took the editorial job in Warsaw, halfway between his home and the Academy, and commuted to Łódź once a week, seeing his wife and children even less often. He had no friends or relatives in Warsaw and lived in a workers' hostel; his life seemed to be devoid of any normal joys or comforts. Before long I could see that he was virtually starving. Yet, this offshoot of genteel poverty, the son of a village schoolteacher, struggled to fulfil his aspirations with indomitable willpower.

In the office Marek always worked hard, never allowing his worries to interfere with his duties. Thoughtful and experienced both about film and as regards life in general, he was a real asset to the Script Bureau. I learned a great deal from him, and he in his turn valued my ideas. Sharing our work, experience and thoughts, we soon became good friends. Sometimes I invited him home secretly intending to share with him the little food we had. Marek and Konrad also got on very well.

Despite his undeniable qualities, Marek did not seem to be much favoured by his superiors. They showed little sympathy for his situation and looked upon him with some distrust. Wojtek Gruda, too, said he knew all about Marek and didn't like him.

Once he told me not to trust him too much and to keep some confidential papers locked away. Although Marek was a Party member, he said, his past was far from exemplary – there was a skeleton hidden in his cupboard.

I could hardly believe his words. As far as I was concerned, Marek was an honest man and a true socialist, one of the few I had known with the same high principles as Konrad's. His character and behaviour were quite different, though. He was an introvert – quiet, retreating, outwardly shy. He rarely spoke at Party meetings, but when he did, what he had to say was always very profound and showed what a deep concern he had for people as well as for work and for the country. The same concern and wisdom was apparent in the reports he wrote about the scripts. No, I couldn't possibly imagine he had anything to hide.

It was Marek himself who finally told me about 'the skeleton in his cupboard', once we had got to know each other well enough to talk about it. Just before the end of the war he had joined the Polish army, straight from a partisan squad he had commanded. For distinguished action (Marek never told me what he had done), he was made captain and soon, though still very young, was then promoted to the rank of major and put in charge of a particularly important unit. I couldn't imagine Marek in a military uniform, Marek in command of soldiers, Marek giving orders to anyone. Yet this was the truth, though it was for only a short period in his life. After two years or so, he was suddenly demoted, deprived of his rank and discharged from the army. The reason for such a severe punishment seemed unbelievably trivial. Before the war Marek had as a child belonged to the Polish Scouts. After the war this organisation was blacklisted by the new regime. Marek had never thought of mentioning his youthful involvement to his superiors. So, when they somehow dug it out, he was accused of concealing his political past. And this was a very serious sin. This was the skeleton in Marek's cupboard for which he was to be punished till the end of his life, it seemed.

Once I had heard Marek's story, I began to respect and trust him even more. Part of my work as an executive of our Party organisation was to deal with all sorts of personal problems amongst its members. I was thus in a position to do something for Marek. He badly needed a flat in Warsaw so that he and his family could finally live together. By then the rebuilding of the city was in full swing – brand-new housing estates were shooting up like mushrooms after heavy rain. But there was still a terrible housing shortage. Every state institution had its own assignment of flats to be allotted to employees according to need and rank. I made repeated attempts to get Marek's name on the list of those urgently in need of a flat, but his applications were constantly turned down. I went to see high-up people but they only shrugged their shoulders: they weren't going to get involved in helping someone with a dubious past. Marek suffered in silence.

When Marek joined the staff at the Script Bureau, my trips to the Łódź Studio became even more useful and fun. We went there together on the days he was exempt from work on the account of his studies. He showed me round every nook and cranny of the Studio and explained everything I needed to know about film making. Once we spent a whole day watching the shooting of some scenes from the film *Five Boys From Barska Street*. I was specially interested in this film as I had read the typescript of the novel it was based on before it was published, and had later recommended it to the film director Aleksander Ford. Ford was a pillar of the Polish cinema at that time. He had been known for his socially committed films well before the war and in the late forties had become famous in Poland and abroad for his film *Border Street* – the first film to show the plight of the Warsaw Jews during the German occupation. The script of *Five Boys* held no great promise, but as Aleksander Ford was screening it, the film was expected to be a major event.

In the biggest of the Studio's shooting halls set for an important scene, above a host of cameras and reflectors, over the busy throng of actors and crew members, a tiny little man hidden behind a big moustache and thick lenses hovered at the top of a huge crane, shouting brisk orders through a loudhailer. The orders sounded like military commands and were carried out at once by his two senior assistants who bustled around at the bottom of the crane. Marek had known these two fellows well and led me straight to them through the labyrinth of props and equipment. But they only smiled politely – they were far too busy and important to chat.

Rooted to the spot at the closed door of the shooting hall stood a pleasant-looking lad dressed in an open-collared shirt and white shorts – the great man's junior assistant. He was in charge of a little crowd of extras waiting outside – from time to time he opened the door to let some of them in, and then closed it again. Seeing us lost in the chaos of the rehearsal he waved and we went over to ask him some questions. Only then did I notice that he was about my age, not at all a boy. Marek introduced him to me as a fellow student from the film Academy and said he would soon be finishing his studies with his own full-length diploma film. Later, when we left the young man, Marek said: 'Remember him. You'll be sure to hear about him sooner or later.' We all heard about Andrzej Wajda two years later when his diploma film *The Generation* gained instant recognition in Poland and throughout the world.

*

It's now over thirty years since I first met Wajda and I still follow his fame from afar. His films are shown sometimes in Britain on television and in the cinema – his famous *Kanal* and *Ashes and Diamonds*, both very close to my heart as I was around when they were being made; the famous *Man of Marble*, produced long after I had left Poland but still 'mine' because I was involved in its long and tortuous story. When in the fifties a young author brought the script of *The Man of Marble* to our Bureau, I was the one who said that though it had great literary qualities it was not suitable for filming because it focused too much on the bleak and disheartening aspects of Polish life. The actual decision to shelve this outstanding script for many years was not mine but I still feel badly about what I said. Yet, both Konrad and I felt deeply moved when, sitting in front of the TV set in our English home, we re-lived our own youthful hopes and disenchantments that we shared with *The Man of Marble*.

In the spring of 1954 Konrad finished his studies and gained his MA degree. Soon afterwards he was appointed junior lecturer in the Faculty of Philosophy and Social Sciences at the University of Warsaw. By then he had changed a great deal. Ever since he had left the army he seemed to see things more clearly. Though still a sincere socialist – which deep in his heart he has remained to this day – he now began to see that all was not right in this world of his. He became more and more aware of contradictions between words and deeds. Perhaps Marxist theory itself, conceived a century ago in different historic and social conditions, needed a new interpretation in our modern times and changed society? Perhaps the duty of a communist who happened to be a scholar was to point his finger at what was wrong, to raise doubts, to rethink ideas which were clearly unworkable? Daily arguments with his university friends and colleagues helped to clarify his mind. His first critical essays followed. He was no longer a blind worshipper of the Party line.

With his widening outlook, Konrad's attitudes towards people gradually began to change too. The first outcome of this change was a reconciliation with his father. One day he went to see his parents to ask for their forgiveness. Like most parents in the world, they were not vindictive – they forgave him at once. So with our family bonds quickly restored, we now visited the old couple every Sunday. They never came to see us, however, as they couldn't bear the idea of entering a guarded military zone. Besides, Zofia was too frail to go anywhere apart from the restaurant where she was still working.

As Konrad was now working again, our bleak spell of living from hand to mouth came to an end. His junior lecturer's salary was nowhere near what he had earned in the army, but it still brought us considerable relief. For me it also meant more freedom: I could now afford to employ someone to take care of Lena whenever I needed to go away. So the following summer I left home for a couple of weeks to spend time on location and have a closer look at the work of a film crew.

The crew were living in a country hotel in a beautiful village on the edge of a vast lake in the west of Poland. I shared a bedroom with the actresses and other female members of the crew and worked during the day like everyone else – I had no wish to be an idle spectator, so for a hot summery fortnight I turned from a script editor into a script-girl. My job was to keep a strict record of every scene shot, standing next to the cameraman and moving around with him whenever he moved.

The working day started early and lasted as long as daylight permitted. There were long spells of idleness when the sun refused to emerge from behind a cloud. There were hordes of horses galloping alongside the lake filmed by the cameraman from a fast-moving car. There were romantic close-ups of the central couple whispering their dreadful lines at sunset. There was a sinister spy creeping through the flowering shrubs, and a greedy kulak who blackmailed a brave party activist. All these major parts were played by mediocre actors. We were making one of the last Polish soc-realistic films.

In the evening, or when rain disrupted the daily schedule, the crew sat around together, usually drinking heavily. Plied with vodka, showered with endearments, and now and again squeezed in the semi-darkness, I tried to feel at my ease. But it was all a pretence – I did not belong there.

It's amazing how much one can learn from sharing someone's work, even if the results are poor. After two weeks as a script-girl I returned home aware that I'd learnt a lot about filming. I now felt an urgent need to put down on paper my thoughts about how a literary work is turned into a film. I also longed to study again, to get better qualifications and a higher degree. Konrad was now far ahead of me, he had already started his doctoral research, and I wanted very much to bridge the gap between us.

It seemed a good time to start studying again. Konrad and I were both settled in jobs and the business of combining work and family was no longer such an ordeal – everything went smoothly. It took me several months to make plans and enquiries and prepare myself for a new challenge. In February 1955 I sat a competitive entry examination and was admitted to a part-time

MA diploma course at the University of Warsaw. I already decided on my project for my thesis. My tutor was very enthusiastic about it and it was accepted at the beginning of May. Three days later a doctor confirmed that I was pregnant.

· 8 ·

I rarely ring Monika these days, knowing she is so busy. Even if I don't ring, I know she is near. Or she may suddenly call on a surprise visit, her ancient red car showing through the hedge. Like a gust of fresh air she bursts into the quiet of our ageing house, her black eyes sparkling, her black hair wind-blown, her black and red clothes in a stylish confusion. She curls up in a comfortable chair and nibbles at biscuits talking about her work. We hear all about the new building she has designed and how it is going steadily up; about the lonely old women who are waiting to make their homes in this new house; about the building workers who used to make fun of her as a pretty lass but have now stopped joking and have a great respect for her.

And here she sits again, my architect, but she looks tired and sad. There's no light in her plum-like eyes, her slacks hardly hide the heaviness of her swelling body.

'How did you cope with it, Mama?'

And here I begin my old tale that she has heard so many times before: three little children . . . full-time work . . . studies . . . Political commitments . . . A constant need to hurry. Sleepless nights. Exhaustion. Yes, things did go wrong sometimes, but somehow it all worked out.

She listens agog as though she were hearing this story for the first time. It sounds new to her. She may find herself in the same position. Will she prove strong enough to cope?

Shall I tell her that my life then was an endless compromise? Yes, I have to tell her that. 'But was it worthwhile?' she asks.

How can I answer this question? After all these long years and bitter disappointments I still can't say 'No'. How sad and dull old age must be for those who cannot recall their youth as a time of faith, of struggle, of ambition? Yet, Monika's feeling of guilt towards her own child, at first suppressed by the sheer joy of living fast, may surface later in her life and gnaw at her heart till the end of her days. Should I tell her this, too? No, I have no right to, she must find her own way.

And here she smiles again, my confident Monika. She knows that everything will be all right in the end.

*

The house was made of red brick and stood in a long row of identical red-brick houses in a recently built housing estate on the outskirts of Warsaw. For centuries this remote suburb of Bielany had been a favourite spot for Sunday family outings, before the postwar crisis forced the authorities to turn it into yet another residential area. It bore all the signs of haste and economy. The new walls already showed cracks, doors and windows did not fit, the courtyard where crowds of children were to have played was a desert devoid of any greenness or beauty. The brand-new estate looked sordid and drab. Nonetheless, we were overjoyed to be given a flat there.

Six years had passed since my first pregnancy and during that time both Konrad and I had matured and were better prepared for parenthood. We were trying to make proper arrangements for our growing family well in advance. It took several months and major efforts to get a new home. Finally, with the help of the university, Konrad was allocated this enviable flat, and in September 1955, with a huge sigh of relief, we moved away from the barracks, leaving all memories of our military past behind.

The new flat was no better than the old one: the two rooms were only slightly bigger and were just as dark – the flat was on the ground floor and faced north. The kitchen had no window at all. The place was also miles away from everywhere else. For years I had been able to walk to work. Now I had to travel daily from the northern end of the city to its southern-most part and back – three hours a day travelling. There was no direct line so I had to take a bus and then change onto a tram. This meant long waiting in a draughty square and then being pushed and shoved about by the impatient crowd.

Since there was no question of me giving up my career after I had the new baby, we found a proper nanny who was to start work shortly before the birth. Lena was sent to a nursery school in the neighbourhood.

Frightened by my first experience of childbirth in the austere military hospital where I had been left alone in labour for hopelessly long hours, forbidden to see my husband or my mother, even when Lena was already born, I decided this time to look for a private clinic. There was only one in Warsaw but with the help of my doctor uncles I managed to book a bed there. The clinic was owned by an elderly woman doctor, once a friend and colleague of my grandfather's. She took me into her expert care, refusing to accept any fee from a descendant of a medical family.

So everything seemed to be fine and for the time being I went on with my work and studies as usual. But as time passed my life turned into an ordeal. Daily travel to and from work, long busy hours in the office, studying late at night and on Sundays, all this completely wore me out. My body grew enormous, my legs looked like two heavy sacks and even simple walking was a torture.

The fact that I was expecting twins was discovered only a month before their birth when, alarmed by my condition, the old doctor ordered an x-ray. And there they were – two tiny human shapes nestling close to each other on the x-ray screen. This unexpected news put us in a state of turmoil. It was easy to love two babies in advance, but how were we going to cope with them? Worried and helpless I saw all my hopes and aspirations vanishing. But our greatest anxiety was how our three children would be looked after.

The newly appointed nanny, who was just about to settle in, immediately resigned; she had been prepared to take care of one newborn baby but not of two. Our desperate attempts to find another nanny seemed doomed to failure. We couldn't ask either of our mothers – they were both working. There was no relative, friend or neighbour to whom we could turn for help. We could only count on ourselves.

As if to make my life even harder, I had arranged to take my first MA exam in November – I wanted to get at least this one off my chest before the birth. The next was due in February. So, after working all day in the office, there I was still working away at home in the evening. Don't ask me how I did it, my daughters, I just did: I passed the first exam and promptly started working for the second. The price I paid was an unrelenting feeling of guilt. While I was busy day and night Konrad had to take over the family, though since his days were extremely busy too, Lena, by then six, often had to fend for herself. She soon learned to fry eggs for her breakfast, wash her own pants and socks, do some shopping in the nearby shop. Properly fed but otherwise shamefully neglected, she looked unkempt and tattered.

Konrad's life became hard and joyless too. November 19th was his thirtieth birthday – a day when one tends to brood on the approach of old age. Overwhelmed by my own concerns and deadly tired, I had forgotten all about it. We spent a dreary evening at home without presents, visitors or even a good meal, brooding and worrying about our precarious future.

I stopped travelling to work only when I could no longer walk to the nearest bus stop, and five days later I was admitted to the clinic. The twins might be born any time now but they were in no hurry. So I lay alone on a hard, bare hospital bed in the delivery ward, waiting for pains and swotting up on the history of philosophy.

With the help of a surgeon, two unusually large and healthy girls joined humanity late one December night, shortly before Christmas. Dazed from the anaesthetic and burning with puerperal fever I hovered in a strange world between life and death. Now and then the gentle, softly spoken nuns in their stiff, white bonnets would silently appear and disappear with a rustle of their long habits. They would bring me my babies and promptly take them away, while I lay numb and listless. Days and weeks passed. The little girls thrived in the loving care of the kindly nuns. The best Warsaw consultants were called for to give advice on my predicament and prescribe new treatments. Week after week with these consultants' urgent letters Konrad rushed to the Ministry of Health and knocked at the doors of the autocrats of the medical world to beg their permission to buy all sorts of antibiotics which were new at that time in Poland and for this reason strictly limited. Then he would queue for hours in an overcrowded pharmacy to buy these latest medicines at fantastic prices. He almost stopped work and for the first time in his life ran into debt. He sat downcast at my bedside, brightening up only when the two plump, bald, dark-eyed babies were brought into the ward.

When after six weeks I was still no better, Konrad finally made up his mind to take my fate into his own hands. At his request I was discharged from the clinic together with my babies who I was still unable to take care of on my own. Konrad now took charge of our whole life. Already breadwinner, cook, nanny, cleaner and washerman, he now became my doctor. With his contempt for the luminaries of the medical profession and his suspicion of all private arrangements, he sought a communal doctor's advice. This modest, obscure but thoroughly experienced man told him what to do: Epsom salts and hot compresses, which Konrad applied to my inflamed breasts with the toughness of a former soldier. These two remedies did the trick, everything that the great consultants and sophisticated medicines could not accomplish, and within a week I was rid of my persistent infection, although not ready yet for normal life.

*

I watch him now, bent over his photographs, my protector, my friend, my love. His hair has turned grey, his face bears signs of a hard life, but his eyes are the same: they still burn with passion. Busy all day with his teaching, he still finds the time, strength and will to work on his new art. It came so late in his busy life, he feels he has to hurry. So, even after a tiring day, he stays up late at night to add a final touching to his unusual prints.

Dripping wet from wash, the photographs show the austere beauty of the Yorkshire landscape, a beauty of stillness and solitude. How does he see such sadness among those green valleys and hills? And why does he search for it?

*

It was Konrad who stayed up at night to feed our two babies. Bending over their cot, he held a bottle of milk in either hand, waiting patiently till they were empty. Later, he would often wake to change their nappies, while I stayed in bed, sleepless but unable to move. The girls were hard work. They were noisy and demanding. They cried a lot at night – Monika in a high-pitched hysterical soprano, Sylvia plaintively like a bleating lamb. Lena shared their bedroom and joined in the chorus full of pity. We soon had to move her into our room and there she slept for over a year.

The winter was fierce, the days very short. In the cold dark mornings Konrad would bend over the bath and wash dozens of nappies. There was no means of drying them in our small, freezing flat, so they had to be hung out in the courtyard. This annoyed some of our neighbours and Konrad had to face them alone. Then he took Lena to her nursery school and collected her eight hours later. In the meantime, he lectured, supervised his students, worked on his doctorate and argued at political meetings. He also did all the shopping, waiting in endless queues.

I stayed at home alone looking after my little girls and studying. I was not yet strong enough to do anything else. In the evening streams of friends invaded our home and lavished praise on the twins: indeed they were growing fast and becoming very pretty. My feelings finally came back and I could express my love for them.

The hard winter was drawing to an end and with it my maternity leave. It had been extended from three to four months because of my illness, but this was now at an end too. There was no way we could find help with the babies and there was no creche anywhere nearby, so I was about to give up my career. But then, thanks to the great goodwill of my superiors, a final decision was postponed till October: I was offered six months' leave without pay. The summer that followed that wintry gloom I remember as a very happy time. I was fit and strong again and I could cope with all sorts of things at once. I managed to pass two of my MA exams and became happily absorbed in family life. When Konrad began his long summer holidays we shared all the daily jobs and had a lovely time with the children – now properly tended, sun-tanned and pampered. Without my salary we were poor, but there was very little in the shops we wanted to buy anyway. Every Saturday evening Konrad's parents would arrive at our remote suburb driven in Zofia's official car. They always brought a basketful of food and stayed for the night, taking over all responsibility for their three granddaughters. So, once a week, Konrad and I could go out and feel young and light-hearted again. After an evening of seeing new films, meeting friends and walking in the streets, we looked forward to the future, especially as things seemed to be changing for the better in the country.

That spring, in a speech given at the Twentieth Congress of the Soviet Communist Party, Khruschev denounced, albeit half-heartedly, the atrocities of Stalin's rule and gave a selected yet shattering catalogue of his crimes. Communists all over the world were dumbfounded. The Polish leader, Bierut, died of a heart attack. At the Party organisation meetings loud voices of shock and anger resounded. At first tentatively but then more and more boldly, the media began to express critical views. As always, the intellectuals were first to move. The Warsaw university seethed. Young scholars and students did not hide their outrage and publicly made major political demands. Konrad's faith, already shaken before, now underwent a crucial change.

But it was the workers who delivered the final blow to the old regime. At the end of June the workers of the Poznan factories marched out into the streets calling for bread and freedom. The demonstration was dispersed with gun-fire and arrests followed. But from now on change was unstoppable.

Official attitudes towards the Western world began slowly to thaw and more visitors were allowed in from capitalist countries. Konrad's sister, Tova, who had tried for years to get a Polish visa, finally succeeded and was coming from Israel for a short visit.

Konrad and his parents had not seen her for seventeen years and had almost lost hope of ever seeing her again. For me too the meeting was very important – I felt I knew her so well from everything I had been told about her and I loved her in advance. Besides, this was the first chance for all of us of a close encounter with someone from a different world.

On the day of Tova's arrival, Konrad travelled to the frontier to meet her on the train; I stayed at home to get everything ready. We had all imagined a woman wasted by hard labour in arid fields; burnt by a merciless sun; exhausted from raising four children; wearing shabby clothes shared by the kibbutz community; longing for better food and culture. I washed and ironed my best Sunday dress planning to give it to my sister-in-law. I spent a whole week's money on early strawberries and tomatoes, luxuries we would not afford for ourselves.

And then she arrived, so brilliant and attractive, so full of energy, so much like her brother. Her beautiful cotton dress was a dream: it did not need ironing! Her suitcase contained fine cosmetics and smart nylon underwear, she was surrounded with a haze of delicate perfume. She ate little, being careful not to get fat, and did not touch my tomatoes: she was sick and tired of them, she said, they grew plenty of them on her kibbutz and had them daily with every meal. All this sounded like a fairy tale.

During her three-week stay Tova told us all about her life. How, soon after coming to Palestine, she had left her first husband and joined the new kibbutz. How, with her second husband and other comrades she had worked in the fields from dawn to dusk, living rough and half starving. How, during the Arab war, armed with rifles, she and other kibbutz women had stood guard by night while their children slept in bunkers. And how with the passing years her kibbutz had grown strong and prosperous, as its members shared work, crops and daily life.

Starry-eyed, I gazed at Tova, lost in admiration. Hers was a meaningful life, a life of commitment to an important cause. She lived for a noble aim, she struggled, shared and belonged. Did I? Yes, of course I did – I had made my decision to stay in Poland and I had not been idle. I had worked as hard as I could for the well-being of *my* country. And I was no longer alone, I had my comrades, my colleagues, my friends who shared my enthusiasm. Yes, I belonged, too. There was no reason to feel inferior. Or was there?

Tova was soon gone. She left me restless. I found it harder than ever to bear my compulsory seclusion. Somewhere outside my stifling flat, far away as well as quite near home, people were struggling to change the course of history. All I was doing was washing nappies and looking after my very private babies. Konrad no longer spent much time at home: he became passionately involved in political struggle which was growing daily more intense. I longed to be back at work and active again in the Party. Instead, I was just about to lose my job, since it was nearly October and there was still no solution to my family problems.

Rescue came unexpectedly in the last week of September. A short, square-built, snub-nosed woman turned up at our door, sent by a friend who knew we needed help. She could start work straight away, even tomorrow, she said – she lived on her own in the same street and liked little children. The ten-month-old twins, standing in their cot on their plump little legs and rocking to and fro, greeted her with broad grins that revealed a total of seven teeth.

So, on the 1st October I travelled back to work again. During my long absence friends from work, who had sometimes visited me, warned me about the major changes that were taking place in the film headquarters, but what I found there on my return went far beyond my expectations. The Script Bureau had ceased to exist, its work dispersed over several recently formed groups of film producers. Marta had gone – she was now working in the budding Polish television world. Marek was in Łódź busy making his diploma film. There was no sign of Wojtek Gruda, he had vanished from sight.

I wandered from one office to another in the huge building, desperately trying to find out what I was supposed to be doing. Nobody could answer this question. The personnel manager assured me that my job and salary were secure since there had been no reason whatever for sacking me. But what my present

duties were he did not know. The secretary of the party organisation – someone new as they had kicked out the previous one –
could not help either. Total chaos reigned in the headquarters,
everything was in a state of transformation. I realised I would
have to look for a job myself.

I found it, or rather one was offered to me, a couple of days
later. Someone in the Programme Department was about to
launch a major new research project into children's perception of
films. To form a proper team he needed a number of graduates
with a sound knowledge of either child psychology or film
language. I fitted into the second category. He begged me to join
his team and waited anxiously for my answer. Three or four
people were already working on a preparatory scheme. Among
them was Diana. She had been demoted from her post as vice-
director of the Documentary Studio when her husband was
purged in disgrace from the public security office. She seemed
tormented and hushed. She smiled faintly when she heard I might
become her colleague. Next day I joined the team. A wide new
field was opening up for me.

Three weeks later, on 24 October 1956, I was standing in the
middle of the huge square outside the Palace of Culture and
Science listening to Gomułka's speech. Lost among the many
hundreds of thousands, I shared the enthusiasm of the crowd.
Half of Warsaw's population seemed to have come here of their
own free will to hail their returning leader, now back after eight
years of persecution and imprisonment. It seemed that – for once
– the nation was united; communists, non-communists and anti-
communists alike; workers, farmers, intellectuals and all.

Well, not all. Gomułka's victory had come after a week of fierce
political fighting. Soviet leaders had arrived to take control and
Soviet troops stationed in Poland had started advancing towards
the capital. Those active in the struggle for change had been
warned to stay away from home at night lest they be arrested.
Konrad was one of them. At the same time, demonstrations by
Hungarian students in Budapest in support of the Polish cause

had turned into a popular revolt that was later to be drowned in blood by the Soviet army. For a week the threat of total disaster had kept us in suspense day and night.

But now the fight was over. Khruschev and his team, temporarily appeased, had returned to the Kremlin and the troops had withdrawn to their barracks. A little grey-faced, withered man without any personal charm or wit stood on the rostrum under the cloudy sky and was cheered by the spellbound throng. We burst spontaneously into a simple birthday song: 'May he live for us one hundred years'.

· 9 ·

Sometimes I go to London – to stay with old friends, to see Sylvia, to run through the galleries. But mainly just to be there. London has never ceased to fill me with both delight and terror. The old fear that I may get lost in its crowded streets never to be found again still wrings my throat for a couple of minutes. The absurd feeling of dumbness, of maladjustment, comes back like a half-forgotten tune.

More than a quarter of a century has passed since the day I saw London for the first time. It all seemed so strange then, so different, so utterly puzzling. The green lawns – after the dullness of the Warsaw streets still dank in the freezing grip of an early spring; the colourful trees; the shop windows loaded with colourful goods; the colourful people – my goodness, I'd known only one black man in Warsaw, a student who introduced himself as the 'Negro' on the telephone and who, in the street, was always followed by a flock of fascinated children. Then there were the puzzling sounds: the street singers, an endless hum of foreign speech, an unfamiliar noise of double-decker buses driving on the wrong side of the road and letting passengers in on the wrong side. And the smells, yes, the unknown smells, the pungent fragrance of plenty and want.

The gate to this strange outside world was suddenly opened for us in the late fifties – not flung wide open, but at least stood ajar. At first it affected our loved ones.

Soon after the October turning point, Gomułka gave new

concessions to Jews who wanted to emigrate to Israel. The collapse of the Stalin cult had brought a great resentment against any Jews who had held top posts in the Party and public security. Although like non-Jewish Stalinists they were already purged, a flood of anti-Semitism was now beginning to arouse a shattering sense of insecurity among Jews. Thousands applied from all over the country for permission to emigrate. Gomułka let them go.

So, Konrad's father was finally able to fulfil his life-long dream. In December 1956, after the final stage of her long illness, Zofia died. He moved in with us soon after the funeral and applied for a passport. A mournful, wasted, lonely old man in his late sixties, his only wish now was to die peacefully in the land of his forefathers. For the time being he slept in Lena's empty bed in the twins' room, went to work each morning and returned in the evening with a shopping bag full of food he had queued for on his way home. He never talked much, never complained, never wanted anything for himself. For the first time I realised how dear he had become to me and I started calling him Father, which I had never done before.

The passport was granted in February, and Father began to prepare to leave. Tova was waiting for him with open arms. She said her kibbutz had everything he needed, so he packed just his books and keepsakes and sent them off well in advance. When this was done there was still time left to say goodbye to everything he had loved and taken for granted throughout his long life. I was walking with him one day in the park. Everything was shrouded in a thick cover of fresh, soft snow. He walked in silence, his gaze wandering over the white peaks of the high oak and chestnut trees, his eyes misty with tears. All of a sudden he stopped at a branch weighed down with its frosty load, took a handful of snow and kissed it goodbye. He left in the spring. We thought we'd never see him again.

The next beloved person we had to part with was Sophie, my sister. She had never given up her youthful determination to live in Palestine, and now she was ready to go. During the years when leaving Poland was almost impossible, she had managed to finish her studies, get a master's degree in microbiology, find highly responsible work in a hospital, publish some scientific articles and marry a member of the Warsaw Philharmonic Orchestra – someone we had both known for years and who shared Sophie's beliefs. Their first child was born six months before they left.

We saw Sophie off at the railway station one September evening. The platform swarmed with emigrants and their friends and relatives who had come to say goodbye. Boxes, baskets, bundles of bedding were shuffled to and fro, and stifled sobs broke the mournful silence. The heavy sorrow of exodus was in the air. I sat in the midst of all this chaos on a suitcase, holding my little niece fast asleep on my lap. Sophie and her husband, with Konrad's help, were struggling to force two huge double-basses into the crowded train. I thought anxiously of their precarious future. Then the baby suddenly woke and peered at me with her bright greenish eyes. I burst into tears, knowing I might never see her grow up.

Mother was thinking of leaving for Israel too. Apart from Sophie, there was no reason for her to go. She had a good job and excellent relations with her colleagues and bosses. She was respected and loved by innumerable friends and no longer felt a stranger in her own country. Even her housing problems had been partly solved, as the dreadful Larks had moved away and a friendly family was now living in the shared flat. She still had a handful of relatives in Warsaw, apart from myself and my family. Nonetheless, she decided to follow Sophie who would be starting a new life in a foreign land and might need her help far more than I ever had. Mother had all the necessary papers but finally decided to delay her departure as just at that moment it was I who could not do without her help.

Two months earlier, Konrad had been offered an American grant for a full year's post-doctoral studies at the London School of Economics. This was a rare chance – very few Polish scholars had ever been given such an opportunity. (Later in the sixties many more Polish scholars received foreign grants.) Konrad knew that to say no would be sheer madness. But to accept seemed sheer madness too: it meant a year away from home. Neither he nor I could imagine how we could survive for such a long time without each other and how I could possibly cope on my own with what was already a heavy burden for both of us.

There was little time for debate. Within a week the decision was made: Konrad would go to London. He left, in October, to return only a year later.

Mother moved in with me, for moral support rather than real help. Like myself she had a job and now had to travel a long distance to work and back, which was a great hardship. But having her with me in the evenings and Sundays meant the world to me.

The first few letters from Konrad were sombre. He was terribly lonely. He had found somewhere to live – a basement room, cold, dark and damp. It cost £11 per month out of his £38.5s allowance. He lived on cheese and rough dumplings that he cooked for himself, trying to save money. His English which had been thought good in Poland, in London caused him no end of trouble. But most of all he missed us bitterly.

My life went on somehow, but it was hard and joyless. Day after day I rushed home from work seized with terror that I might be late. The nanny was always waiting in the corridor dressed in hat and coat, ready to go. She would complain rudely if I happened to be late, which was never my fault. I was always at the mercy of overcrowded trams and buses and having to wait in long queues at the shops. However, the fear that I might lose her, the very thought that she might one day go and never come back made me silent and meek. I was totally dependent on her and she knew it.

My three little girls would also be waiting anxiously for me. Lena was now going to school. Totally ignored by the nanny, she badly needed me to take care of her, to listen to her problems and answer her questions. The twins had to be given their evening meal, bathed one after the other, then put to bed and lulled to sleep with a fairy-tale – they already understood and loved fairy stories. Trying to show them the love and patient attention that they all missed so much was perhaps the most difficult thing. I was so exhausted after a hectic day that all I wanted was for them to go to sleep as fast as possible and leave me in peace. I felt constantly guilty of being a callous, inadequate mother. Such guilt has haunted me to this very day.

My job at work was now to summarise findings of our research project. The exciting months of gathering materials when thousands of school-children had been shown scores of films, asked innumerable questions, and closely watched, were over. The team was now attempting to take stock of this vast volume of material. This was a dull, monotonous task requiring a great deal of time and patience. But I could already see that the results would be very interesting. Since I was now working away from scripts and film studios, I had had to give up my original MA research project and I decided to take on the subject of this new research for my thesis.

As the weeks passed by, Konrad's letters gradually became brighter, even cheerful. His English was improving rapidly, his research was going fast and extremely well. He had changed his digs and now lived in a better room, paying a lower rent. At the end of November, with an outburst of unrestrained joy, he announced that he would be able to save enough money for me to make a trip to London. He begged me to do everything I could to find someone good to take care of the children, and to come to London for a full month. This sounded like a fairy tale and – like a fairy tale – seemed totally unreal. There was no one I could entrust my little crumbs to, no one who would even be willing to take them on for me. I began to despair, seeing no way of making this dream come true. But then my romantic mother, who always believed that two people who love each other should be together, made a marvellously generous offer: she would take her holiday leave while I went to London and stay at home with her granddaughters. She hoped the nanny would be more helpful when I was away, which in fact proved right: like everyone else, the nanny adored my mother and did everything she could to please her.

My one thought now was to see Konrad and I did all my daily jobs in a daydream. My life became even more hectic than before as in addition to everything else I had to struggle for a passport and a British visa. This meant frequent visits to the Ministry of the Interior and to the British Embassy, and long hours of waiting in those two most unpleasant places. At the Ministry they treated all passport applicants with utmost suspicion as though they were potential defectors to the West; at the Embassy they saw us as beggars who, once allowed entry, might try to stay in Britain for ever. Three months went by before I obtained my Polish passport with its coveted British stamp. On that day two delirious telegrams were exchanged between Warsaw and London and the date of my arrival was fixed for 22 March 1958. I started getting ready for the journey.

Very few of my friends and acquaintances had ever travelled to the West but everyone tried to give me advice. I was forced to buy a pair of ski boots and a hat that I never wore; I was offered a three-metre-long string of sausage – a rarity in the Warsaw shops – to live on in London. I was advised to take two bottles of vodka, just in case. On the day of my departure a little crowd of excited well-wishers gathered on the platform and, when I was already on the train, someone came running to hand me a pound of lemons, another rarity in Warsaw; I was supposed to eat them on my way.

The journey took thirty-six hours and was a nightmare. Crammed in a compartment with a group of people who were emigrating to Britain to join their sons, brothers or husbands who had lived there since the Second World War, I could hardly stir for all the bundles of bedding. When we arrived in the middle of the night at the Polish-German frontier, the two respective teams of soldiers and custom officers searched the train in turn, looking for runaways and ripping open pillows and feather quilts. Even my tiny travelling cushion was cut open in case I was smuggling gold.

I spent the following night on a British ferry between the Hook of Holland and Harwich. Konrad had sent me some shillings and pence so that I could afford a feast: sitting in an elegant bar on the upper deck I sipped grapefruit juice through a straw and considered myself a woman of the world. But next morning, when I woke in the shared lower-deck cabin, all the gloss of this wide free world was gone. An irritated steward pushed his way through the little crowd of Polish emigrés gathered in the passage shouting in English and forcing everyone to have morning tea. Unable to understand and bewildered, the passengers meekly picked up cups of horrid, tepid, whitish liquid from his tray. When the tray was empty, the rude man began to roar even louder, demanding tips. As I was the only one in the crowd who could understand him, he turned on me with an order to translate his demand into Polish. At that moment, I hated the capitalist West with all my heart.

The last trying experience awaited me in Harwich. The passport officer could not or did not want to speak French, so I had to humiliate myself by explaining the purpose of my visit to Britain in my disgraceful English.

At nine o'clock the same morning I arrived at Liverpool Street Station, the place I had been longing to see for the last five months. Konrad was already waiting there. He was dressed in a new plastic anorak and held a bunch of tulips. I burst into tears, he looked so thin and frail: he had been starving himself all that time to pay for my trip.

In a black taxi, reminiscent of a funeral car, we travelled to Archway through a tangle of innumerable North London streets. Mad from joy and from lack of sleep I could note only that everything around seemed bustling, colourful and abundant.

Throughout this unforgettable month, which we called our second honeymoon, I kept a journal, jotting down from time to time only what struck me most.

Sunday 23rd March 1958
Konrad says we are living in one of the poorest parts of London. But it's hard to believe this: everything looks so colourful and gay. The people can't really be poor if they own their own little houses. Our attic room, which Konrad rents from a worker's family, is lovely: bright, flowery wallpaper; a sloping ceiling hanging low over an antique bed; a tiny window overlooking a little back garden; two well-worn armchairs facing a gas heater framed by a

wooden mantelpiece – it's all so cosy, so unusual. The only snag is it's freezing cold unless we turn on the heater. Which we do only from time to time, pushing the large one-penny coins into a special slot. We're sadly aware of burning up Konrad's grant, so we only buy ourselves short spells of warmth.

This morning our landlady came to say hello. She seems extremely friendly. She offered to take our laundry to her new washing machine. Washing machine, what a luxury! At the same time she says that she and her husband only go to the West End once a year, to celebrate her birthday. They can't afford it more often. But we, who wouldn't dream of buying a washing machine, went to the West End last night.

In Soho: multi-coloured crowds, the sharp smells of fried meat, an air of shady excitement. Prostitutes: they don't solicit, they just stand there propped against the walls, waiting. I felt sorry for them. The Salvation Army – characters straight from an operetta – try to save the fallen women's souls and fill the street with their ear-splitting music. Bright neon lights advertise all sorts of worldly goods and pleasures, the mythical Coca Cola most of all. We landed in a music hall called The Prince of Wales, a place where the usherettes show all their long legs in net stockings. The audience sit with their coats on, smoking and making loud remarks during the performance. Lots of black men. Coca Cola again, advertised on the stage curtain. The performers: Miss Glamour – a strikingly attractive mulatto; Sabrina – someone with incredible breasts that jut out horizontally for thirty centimetres at least. Throughout the performance stark naked women on the stage – they don't perform, they stand still all the time because British censorship thinks it's less offensive. There were lots of songs, sketches and jokes which I couldn't understand, but Konrad says they were all in very bad taste. The audience split their sides with laughter. We travelled back on the tube – something of an Orpheus in the Underworld.

Monday 24th March 1958

This morning a grocery shop round the corner. No queues, no crowds, we just walked in. In ten minutes we bought thirty-seven items, going round with a wire basket and scooping up whatever we fancied from the shelves. It's called 'self-service', a marvellous invention. The plenty, the choice, the display of food are breathtaking. Meats and cheeses of all possible kinds are already cut into neat, small or large sizes and wrapped in cellophane with weights and prices shown on the tops of the parcels. One just picks them up from a refrigerated counter. We spent a fortune of £2 1s but what a feast for a whole week at least!

Tuesday 25th March 1958

Very cold. We walked in Waterlow Park, straight on the beautiful lush lawns. At first I was frightened we might be fined for trampling the grass, as we certainly would have been in Warsaw. But it's allowed here, everyone takes it for granted. Lots of little children around. Amazing how they treat them. Despite the bitter cold, young toddlers travel half-naked in their high, black, mournful-looking prams. Bare little heads, bare little legs everywhere. There were twins, too, settled comfortably in a special pram with twin hoods, one opposite the other. Why can't we have something like that?

Then Hampstead – rich people's world. Smart, individual houses each of a different shape, style and charm. Flowers in full bloom in front of the houses. Privacy. Splendid isolation. Groceries delivered to the back door. Tangible prosperity. All this after what we saw last night in Soho: those homeless, tattered, hairy tramps, men and women sleeping rough on the pavements.

Wednesday 26th March 1958

Since I said Archway was in fact a nice place to live, Konrad has wanted to show me a truly squalid part of London, so we travelled to Stepney. But Stepney which he said was once a place of most abject poverty, practically doesn't exist any longer: the filthy old buildings are just being pulled down. A vast, deserted space, covered with rubble and debris. It immediately reminded me of the Warsaw ghetto just after the war. Strangely enough, in the midst of all this wilderness, we found a pub that was still open. We walked in and ordered a drink called shandy. There were only three other customers, all of them old women looking destitute and forlorn. Apparently they go there only because there is nowhere else in the whole world for them to keep warm and talk. Whatever we think about Poland with all her shortcomings and faults, we should be proud and happy to live there. There are neither tattered old women sleeping rough in the streets, nor idle, fur-coated ladies driving their luxury cars along the same streets. Everything is drab in our country, but everyone shares in the drabness to more or less the same extent.

Thursday 27th March 1958
In Hyde Park a funny bearded man with a patched cape hanging down from his meagre shoulders stood on an empty box and at the top of his hoarse voice publicly cursed the British government. A few passers-by stopped and listened. A tall, smart policeman stopped to listen, too, then peacefully walked away. All agog, I waited for something terrible to happen. But nothing did. Incredible.

Friday 28th March 1958
Woolworths. I couldn't resist the temptation and bought two lovely bright-coloured plastic sponges – one for Mother, one for myself. I feel a little guilty at being so greedy.
Natural History Museum: dinosaurs, diplodoci, ichtiosaurs, plesiosaurs, archaeopteryxes, whale.

Saturday 29th March 1958
All-night party at Laurie's from the LSE. About fifty people squeezed into the semi-darkness, standing, talking,

drinking. No food, only wine and other drinks which they sip slowly all the time. No toasts, no 'bottoms-up'. Bowls with little crunchy things scattered everywhere: they munch non-stop. A bedroom upstairs turned into a cloakroom. Among the coats and hats deposited on the beds – bags with sleeping babies. Shocking.

After several glasses of sherry I discovered I could speak English, so I talked a lot, mainly answering questions, such as: 'Do you have running water in Warsaw?' or: 'Is it safe to speak Polish in the street?' There was a bloody reactionary among the guests whom I would gladly have strangled for what he thought about Poland. But on the whole the people I talked to were homely and very kind, though totally confused about life on the other side of the 'Iron Curtain'.

Monday 7th April 1958
I can hardly keep these notes up to date: so much is going on during the day and when I finally land in bed, I'm too sleepy to write. We saw lots of wonderful things last week, but who can describe the National Gallery, the Tate Gallery, or the British Museum? We went to a concert in the Royal Festival Hall, too, and have seen six films which I intend to write an article about when I get back home.

What I terribly enjoy here is travelling through London on the buses. We always sit at the front on the top deck, smoke 'Bristols' (1s 8d a packet – a sheer delight compared to what we smoke at home), and look down at the changing streets. It's as exciting as seeing a good film.

Thursday 10th April 1958
I'm fed up with luxury, with the abundance of goods for sale. We went shopping today. Marks and Spencer was fun at first. I browsed in a heap of blouses (£1 each) and nobody stood at my back to keep an eye on me. I chose two, very nice ones, and can still change them if I wish, or return them and get my money back. But I won't. I bought a pleated skirt, too – £4. It doesn't need dry cleaning, it

doesn't need ironing, it looks indestructible. I'll be smart for the rest of my life. But there was such a lot of everything, such a multitude of beautiful clothes one would like to buy that I quickly got tired of looking at them and felt greatly relieved when we left the store.

Then we went to Harrods. Konrad only wanted to show me this place, knowing that he wouldn't be able to buy anything there. Indeed . . . Those fur coats, those porcelain sets, those leather armchairs . . . Precious jewellery . . . I was stunned, but not out of greed: I could easily be tempted by a pretty dress, but never by a mink jacket or diamond ring. In the end Konrad couldn't bear being just a window shopper and suddenly decided we would buy something after all. What? A piece of cheese. We were just approaching an immense circular counter loaded with a thousand exquisite cheeses from all over the world. A formidable man, dressed in a white overall and stiff white headgear, stood behind the counter like a soldier on guard. I could swear he gave us a scornful glance when Konrad asked for a Camembert. Negligently, he reached for a wooden box, lifted the lid and abruptly pointed the open box at me. I was so frightened that my legs began to tremble. I had no idea what he expected from me. But Konrad knew and whispered in Polish: 'Touch it,' which I did. 'Say it's all right.' I said it was all right. 'Thank you, Madam,' said the formidable man with a malicious grin and wrapped the damned Camembert in a beautiful sheet of paper. Never, never again.

Wednesday 16th April 1958
I'm ready for home. I can't wait to see the children, Mother, friends. To speak Polish and sound intelligent again. But mainly perhaps to stop feeling guilty about all the people sleeping rough, and to get away from the scornful glances of the worshippers of wealth. If only I could take Konrad with me! And a few other things: a washing machine, a self-service shop, the National Gallery, freedom of speech, trust

. . . yes, trust – in this country they don't see you as a thief or a crook unless you behave as one. It will be hard without this back home. But I do belong there.

I no longer belonged there when, thirteen years later, I came back to England to make it my home. But neither did I belong here. At first, I lived in a vacuum, rooted nowhere, bound to no anchor. It was a bad time for all four of us. The first year . . . The second year . . . Konrad, as the breadwinner, suffered most, bearing the burden and heat of the day. Only slowly, very slowly, did he come to terms with his new role and his new surroundings. But at least he did belong to a certain place right from the start, being anchored to the Department and defined as its head. The girls found it very hard indeed. Coming to England was none of their choice: they were only fifteen and had to go along with what we decided. They were taken away from their Israeli school where they had only just settled down, put on a ship and brought to this foreign place – where they had to start all over again. They had no proper knowledge of English; there were huge gaps in what they were supposed to know in a British school; they had no friends. We arrived in Leeds on 1st July, and two months later they went to a good grammar school in the neighbourhood. At first their position there was vague. They were old enough to go into the fifth form, but it was impossible to think of them taking their 'O' level exams by the end of the school year. At least this was what their teachers said. But to put them in the fourth form with younger girls would have broken their spirit and ruined their determination to work. We felt this was a real threat so we decided to talk to the headmistress.

The headmistress was an overpowering woman, noble but rigid in appearance. I felt like a pupil myself in her presence and didn't dare open my mouth. Konrad felt exactly the same, but summoned up all his courage to speak his mind. He succeeded: the headmistress was wise and experienced, and took his point at once. The twins went into the fifth form. Now it was up to them to prove their father right.

They set about this straight away, wasting no time. It was all work – work after classes, work at night, work at the weekends and on holiday. When the 'mock' examinations came in December the teachers were amazed to see how well they had done in such a short time. All the same, they said, there was little hope the girls would get anywhere in June.

That first winter of tension and gloom turned into a hectic spring. June came and the examinations began. The girls tried really hard and their final successes surpassed all our expectations: Sylvia passed seven 'O' levels, Monika eight. But the enormous stress and strain they had lived under for almost a year took its toll. Monika fell ill with a serious illness; Sylvia, though physically fit, began a long period of depression. I remember her going through the last two years of high school withdrawn, languid and subdued, no smile ever brightening her pale face and amber-coloured eyes. Silent and shy, always looking to her twin sister for protection, and hiding in her shade, she led a miserable life.

*

I often wonder how it happened that the most vulnerable of my children chose to live in a city that fills my soul with awe. One day Sylvia went to London and found happiness there. With the passing years she has become an artist. She is no longer shy. From room to room in a famous London gallery she moves so freely, so confidently, as though it were her home. Followed by a flock of fascinated strangers, she shows them the masterpieces of art. She tells them tales about the Old Masters, shows the meaning behind the colours and shapes. Her voice is bright, her eyes are smiling, she thrives among those people, between these precious walls.

Back in her attic studio, she sits at an easel and paints her own pictures full of colour and light.

*

While the three of my family were struggling to find a place for themselves in their new surroundings, I was left on my own with no place to go and no clear aim to fight for. Bound only to the house, I automatically became a housewife. I had been a career woman since my early adult life, and this change came as a bitter blow. My only work now was cooking, cleaning and washing so as to keep my hard-working husband and children comfortable and satisfied. I had never liked housework, nor was I any good at it. So I had a lot to learn, the more so as everything in this country was different from what I had been used to. And although I made rapid progress, I still did not find it exciting. Scalding and cutting my fingers, spending long hours on such uncreative jobs as dusting and scrubbing, I racked my brains to find a way out of my cage.

I soon discovered that my status as a housewife not only seemed natural but was also fully acceptable to our new acquaintances. At this early stage of our life in England we were surrounded by kind people wanting to help and make sure we weren't lonely. First of all Konrad's colleagues and then our neighbours called on us with little gifts and helpful hints. A week hardly went by without an invitation to a party or an evening meal. It warmed my heart and I was truly grateful to all these strangers for being so friendly. At the same time, I felt terribly awkward amongst them and not my usual self. Firstly, because of the language. I could hardly avoid speaking when they asked questions and tried to coax me into small talk. But in my tense and painfully self-conscious state, I heard my own voice coming from outside. I was well aware of every mistake I made, every wrong pronunciation, every clumsy expression. I could not help blushing and this made me even more exasperated. I imagined people would think I was totally boring, ill-educated, perhaps even half-witted. I was usually asked questions about Poland, but when I started on a carefully worded answer, people would quickly change the subject or turn to someone else. Being so tactful and gentle, they probably did not want to embarrass me by making me talk. Sometimes, maybe, they were not interested enough to wait for an answer: they knew very little about that strange, eastern European country and did not seem very keen to learn more. At one official party, a VIP's wife came up to make our acquaintance. We were just talking to a visiting American professor and the lady addressed him first: 'Where are you from Professor?' she asked. 'I'm from California,' he answered. 'Oh, how exciting,' exclaimed Mrs VIP, 'It must be lovely to live in California.' She then turned immediately to Konrad: 'Where are you from, Professor?' 'I'm from Poland.' 'Oh, how exciting! It must be lovely to live in Poland.' And off she went to talk to other guests, surely to ask them the same question.

The warm welcome we were receiving from so many people had to be returned. We started giving dinner parties for two or three couples at a time. This was even more exhausting for me than being a guest. I had to be both a hostess, entertaining my guests with intelligent talk, and a cook, producing a good dinner. I knew quite well that English cookery was beyond me, so I decided to serve Polish meals. Armed with special foods from a Polish shop and guided by my well-worn Polish cookery book, I soon achieved splendid results in the field of borsch and bigos. These two dishes – beetroot soup and sauerkraut stewed with meat and sausages, the staple diet of Polish peasants – became the standard fare at our elegant dinner parties. Our visitors enthused about the food and asked for the recipes, but rarely accepted a second helping. It was some time before it occurred to me that they might be hating every mouthful they swallowed. During these dinners I followed every discussion eagerly, usually finding them very interesting, but seldom said a word myself. Sometimes I felt a strong urge to join in on a subject I knew a lot about, but it always took me such a long time to prepare my lines that in the meantime the discussion would have turned to another subject. Even when I managed to chime in just on time, it always sounded flat, not in the least what I wanted to say. So I usually sat silent, feeling an utter failure. Nobody ever asked me what my profession was or what I had done in Poland. I was a wife, a professor's wife and my visitors seemed fully satisfied with that. The only questions they ever asked me were: 'How do you like it here?' or 'How old are your daughters?' Nobody ever asked me what my personal plans were or what I intended to do in this country.

*

Eleven years earlier, in 1960, I finished my research work and the report was published. It was intended for anyone interested in child psychology and those who made children's films. I took my MA degree and soon after got a permanent job again. It was not a new one, in fact: I was back with film scripts doing my favourite reviewing. This time, however, I was a senior consultant working on my own, with no immediate boss, colleagues or clerical help, accountable only to the friendly Programme Director who knew me from my earlier work in the Script Bureau and had invited me to work in his department. To my surprise I found there my old friend Beata from educational scripts. She was now a secretary and loved her work, especially after her many years of drudgery in the film warehouse. We were both very pleased to see each other again, back in the high building in Pulawska Street.

My new job was to act as a link between the film producers and the Deputy Minister of Culture and Art. The Deputy, who out of courtesy we called just Minister, was responsible for general government film policy and had the final word on all matters relating to film scripts, proposed by producers. He was a middle-aged man from a peasant background, a newcomer to the world of art. He had little experience but was very clever and keen to learn fast. However, he needed a lot of help and expert advice. It was me who helped him to appraise the scripts and decide what to do with them. It was usually me who had to convey his decision to the author.

By this time Polish cinema was already famous world-wide firstly because of Wajda's *Generation*, *Kanal* and *Ashes and Diamonds*, and then thanks to many other talented film directors, like Andrzej Munk, Jerzy Kawalerowicz or Wojciech Has. There also was a group of outstanding graduates from the Film Academy, all ready to make their debuts. Among these was Roman Polanski. My friend Marek was on his way up. He was at last recognised as a director of talent and an honest member of the Party. He was given permanent work as a director and a flat in Warsaw.

The two big studios – in Łódź and Wrocław – started producing over twenty full-length feature films a year. Scripts poured in to my office day after day. My position between the two powers – the creative and the administrative – was not at all easy. Some of the writers and producers were very nervous of me – they worried I might advise the Minister against their scripts. The Minister, on the other hand, was a stubborn man and had strong preconceived ideas. Being a devoted Party member he gave top priority to any scripts with a strong ideological component, sometimes failing to see that they were not good. Or he would want to reject a script of enormous promise simply because in his view it fell short as a tool of political education. In the stormy era of great change in October 1956 socialist realism had been condemned and apparently rejected for ever. In the early sixties it seemed somehow to be creeping back.

I belonged to the Party myself and was in no way opposed to thinking in terms of what might support or damage the socialist cause. At the same time, however, I felt strongly that the public would never be swayed by boring, wishy-washy pictures and that true art was something to be cherished, whatever its explicit message – it could never be harmful to socialism. In forming my ideas and writing reports I wanted to be honest with myself and tried never to resort to politicking, to praise what I really liked and criticise what I disliked. The Minister was prudish and petit-bourgeois in his taste. He knew very little about literature or art. But he was keen to improve his knowledge and understanding. I tried to help him fill the most blatant gaps in his knowledge. In my reports I often referred him to literary sources or famous paintings and tried on one pretext or another to lend him a book from my own collection. He appreciated this and had great respect for me. I think he also liked me very much though at that stage of our work together he rarely called me to his office – most of our daily contacts took place in writing.

Although my work was now more prestigious than ever before, my salary stayed the same. Nonetheless, we were as a family gradually becoming prosperous thanks to Konrad. He had finished his post-doctoral research on the British Labour movement soon after his return from London. He had two or three books published already and others well on the way. He was well thought of as an author and publishers were only too keen to commission new works from him. As authors were paid by the line, and paid handsomely, his salary was soon only a small part of his income.

We moved from Bielany halfway to the city centre and to a far better flat. We now had four rooms – three very small and one a little bigger. After all our years of discomfort we were at last able to stretch ourselves out a bit. My long journeys to and from work were cut by half. My exams were over and I had no thesis to write. I was finally able to spend much more time with family and friends.

The twins were now old enough to go to kindergarten and then to school. Lena entered her teens, was a star in her class and a great help at home. The nanny was gone. We now needed someone to run the house for us. But the housekeepers we rather carelessly employed never turned out very well, so more often than not we managed without help. Despite horrible stews put into the oven first thing in the morning and left brewing there all day till our return from work, we were very happy not to have a stranger around at home. Konrad was still in charge of the household, shopping and cooking whenever he could, but we all tried to help out. A bit of untidiness in the flat and running out of food now and again did not bother us much. We bought a television and a noisy washing machine. Then came a second-hand Syrena – an early Polish car that would start only when she cared to. With her help we began to enjoy some adventurous family outings, though we were never sure of getting where we wanted to.

By that time Konrad's father had died, far away, in Tova's kibbutz. My mother had left Poland to live with Sophie and her family. From their new home in the suburbs of Tel Aviv she wrote us long nostalgic letters. We had no close relatives nearby but thrived amidst close friends. We were virtually besieged by people who, like ourselves, were working hard, bringing up young children and rapidly improving their positions in the world and standard of living. Our days were packed with endless work, our nights were spent with friends.

*

Where are those friends today? Of all those who used to be so dear to me only a very few remain. We have made new friends in our new country to replace the old ones.

'Friendship, friends . . . you use these words too often,' says my old friend MS, a person of strict moral judgement. 'You call "friends" people you know very little only because you enjoy spending time with them.' I know she is right but I can't find another word for those people I've grown fond of so late in my life. They are new friends, in a new, English sense. I enjoy meeting them, I feel at ease with them. I know they wish me well and I wish them every happiness for as long as they live. They have their faults, I suppose, but this is none of my business: it doesn't spoil my pleasure in being with them.

With my old friends, in the old, Polish meaning, it is another story. Some very close ones, much cherished ones, washed their hands of us and turned away. Others we deserted when we left the country, losing them for ever. Our old friends who can still be called such, are scattered all round the world and only a very few, a handful, still live close enough for us to see them sometimes. Our old friends are no longer young. They have gone through hard times, and bitter disappointments. They bear heavy scars, but they never give up. They have great virtues and very many faults. I take them as they are, for better or for worse. They are not easy to live with but I love them all.

*

Back in the sixties, we never thought it would all end like this: with betrayals and partings . . . We lived a full, happy life and had a strong sense of belonging. At work I felt ever more appreciated and respected and this feeling was after a time clearly confirmed by an unusual offer. One day the Minister called me to his office and asked whether I would be prepared to represent Polish Film at the International Film Festival in Locarno, as the head of the delegation. Amazed, I timidly said yes. My agonising doubts came only when I left the room.

I had a month in which to prepare myself for this demanding, responsible assignment. My days became ghastly, my nights sleepless. I couldn't picture myself as the head of any group of people, let alone as the leader of a delegation entrusted with representing their country on such a serious mission. I realised I would have to meet lots of foreign artists, film producers, writers, some of them very famous; answer lots of questions about Polish films and Poland; talk in foreign languages and play the part of a woman of the world, as smart and fashionable as the great stars of international cinema, among whom I would have to move. I feared I could bring shame on my people's republic. Then there was the problem of the team itself. The film chosen for the competition, *Panic on the Train*, was a well made and played moral drama recently completed and not yet shown to the Polish public. Its director, the actress who played the main part, a film critic and a sales manager were the other members of the delegation. I did not know them well enough to be able to tell whether they would like me as their leader.

I used the remaining time to prepare my own person according to the requirements of my new part. I collected all possible information about Polish cinema, brushed up my French, and paid special attention to my clothes. I bought two pieces of beautiful silk – Poland's great pride – and ordered two dresses from my humble but skilful dressmaker, who became terribly excited when she heard why I needed them; I spent a fortune on a stylish little hat and a pair of high stilettos. But my legs were trembling as on the day of our departure I arrived, unusually smart, at the airport.

Once on the plane I realised there was no need to worry as far as the team was concerned. They were all young and not yet spoiled by success. Like myself, they had never before been abroad to represent their country. They were all as nervous as I was and dreaded the days to come. The actress was particularly frightened as she knew no foreign language. She was a charming woman, though, and I was sure everyone would like her. We all became very friendly at once and our long journey was most enjoyable.

Locarno is a famous holiday resort for the rich from all over the world. It lies on the shore of Lago Maggiore in the Italian part of Switzerland. When we arrived there at sunset, the midsummer heat, the abundance of exotic flowers and trees, the great beauty of the lake and the endless rows of magnificent hotels made us feel as though we had left the real world behind us. We were greeted in French by a Festival official, to whom I had to answer and then introduce the members of the delegation. We were then driven in his splendid car to our hotel. It was a little smaller and less magnificent than the others, but still superb by our standards. We all had separate rooms, and I, as the head of the delegation, was honoured with a suite. It was huge – bigger than my whole four-room flat in Warsaw – and consisted of a bedroom, a sitting room and an unbelievably sparkling bathroom where the bath-tub, wash-basin and lavatory seat were shrouded in clean paper sheets announcing in bold type that everything had been thoroughly cleaned for my use. I found in the sitting room a large heap of invitations to forthcoming events: to closed film-shows and to more or less official luncheons, dinners and banquets. That night, falling asleep in an enormous, spotless bed, I began to feel I must indeed be a very important person.

It was hard work, however, as we soon found out on the following day. Scores of films had to be seen, hundreds of people met and talked to, if only briefly. We had to move from one party to another, changing our clothes in between according to the occasion. All this went on in a raging heat and in the vapours of alcohol we constantly drank, either because we had to at parties, or because we wanted to when finally, late at night, we were left on our own. There was very little time for resting, and lack of sleep greatly contributed to a strange feeling of haziness and unreality. I think that is why I have forgotten most of the films I saw in Locarno. The only one I remember clearly was Buñuel's *Viridiana*. It was by far the most brilliant film shown there and it won first prize in the Festival – The Golden Sail. To our astonishment, the second prize – The Silver Sail – went to our own modest film – we were delirious with joy! Before this happened, the strangers we mixed with ignored us almost entirely and we made hardly any contacts with celebrities of the Western cinema. No other country from the Eastern bloc had sent a delegation, though a Czech journalist and the Soviet cultural attaché were taking part as observers. These two men joined us immediately and we became inseparable. They were both fairly young and very easy-going, so we had great fun with them. I spoke Russian with them and only when we parted at the end of the Festival did the attaché say how delighted he was that he had been able to understand my Polish so well. There were also two men from the Polish embassy who kept in constant touch with us. I had an unpleasant feeling of being watched whenever they were around. Luckily, they were seldom invited to the major events, so we were free at such times from their prying eyes.

Once we were invited on a late-night cruise around the lake. We were to meet here the famous Swiss writer, Friedrich Dürrenmatt. I had read and greatly admired everything he had ever written, and the actress had played main parts in his plays in Warsaw. So we both looked forward to meeting him but it was a great disappointment. The famous playwright loitered on the boat half-naked and drunk; he hardly knew who we were or what we were talking about.

Only towards the end of the Festival, when the Polish film won the Silver Sail, were we suddenly discovered and besieged by well-wishers and journalists. We were asked endless questions and photographed non-stop for colour magazines.

The last event we were invited to was an exclusive banquet given by the organisers of the Festival for the most important participants: the prize-winners and the sponsors – the international millionaires. Our friends – the Russian and the Czech –

were also invited, so the seven of us made a headlong advance towards this assembly of capitalist blood-suckers. Rustling in my silks, clattering with my stiletto heels on the shiny parquet, I proudly led my team across the splendid hall full of millionaires. We found our table marked with little flags – Polish, Russian and Czech – and felt at home at once. A swarm of waiters in black tails bustled round, pouring champagne into crystal glasses and serving whole lobsters from silver trays – things we had only ever heard about before. People at the nearby table devoured their food in silence. They glittered with pearls, gold and diamonds. They looked old and bored. This put us in high spirits. We were all young and successful. We were about to go home to our ordinary but satisfying lives. To live without champagne, pearls or the tedium of superfluity. Struggling with the unmanageable lobster shell I felt united with my six companions against all the riches of the Western world. I was in seventh heaven. I belonged.

Soon after my return from Locarno, I suddenly heard from Wojtek Gruda. I hadn't seen him for several years and had almost forgotten about him. He sent me a sentimental letter saying he had seen my photograph in a weekly film magazine, read all about our success at Locarno and realised he had been longing to see me. He begged me to meet him in Łazienki park after work one day.

I was pleased to see him when, at the appointed time, I found him sitting on a bench under an old chestnut tree. He had put on weight over the years and was much paler than before. But to make up for these shortcomings, he had changed his style – instead of wearing an open-neck shirt or casual pullover, he now had on a tailored suit with an impressive tie. Our meeting was a little chaotic and did not last long, because I soon had to rush home, as usual. The conversation faltered, as it often does between people who have not seen each other for many years. There was either too much to say, or too little. Wojtek didn't seem keen to talk much about himself, he seemed to want to hear about my exploits abroad. He wanted to know how I had coped with the foreign press, how the other members of the delegation had behaved, whether we had liked what we had seen in the West. There was nothing in particular to say about all this – besides I didn't want to gossip. I changed the subject and soon said I should be going home. He jumped to his feet and offered to see me to the bus. As we walked through the park, he said he badly missed our old friendship and his own involvement with the artistic world. He now worked in a ministry and this was much less exciting. This was why he always tried to keep in touch with his old mates and in fact he knew quite a lot about things at the Film headquarters. As usual, he sounded a little boastful as he said this with his old air of a man in the know. 'Big changes are brewing over there,' he said. 'Some of the top officials are soon going.' Taken aback, I asked who these officials were, but he was evasive. 'What have they done to deserve dismissal?' I insisted. 'It's not what they've done, but who they are,' he said vaguely. His eyes were blank. My bus pulled up, the conversation was over. I promised Wojtek to phone him as soon as I had time to see him again. I never kept this promise.

A minor purge took place that winter, which for its unusual and long-lasting frost won the name of Winter of the Century. Just before Christmas three departmental directors were suddenly dismissed from their posts and sacked outright from the head-quarters. No reason was ever given. Two of the directors were members of the Party, all three of them had been working there for years and were popular with employees. They had little in common with each other, except for one thing: they were all of Jewish origin. The film milieu seethed with whispered rumours. It seemed clear that the order to sack the three men had come from outside.

In the bitter cold, in an unwholesome excitement that brought all work practically to a standstill, I bewailed my Programme director, one of those sacked. I had worked in his department for so many years and was very fond of him. Bewildered and miserable, he sat in his office, trying to clear it up for his future successor, attended only by his secretary Beata, who could hardly conceal her distress. He had no more idea than anyone else why he had been dismissed. Many of those who had previously queued at his door and scrambled for his favours, suddenly deserted him. He left on Christmas Eve, saying goodbye to no one but the few people who had not turned their backs on him.

When, gloomy and frozen, I returned to work after the short Christmas break, I was immediately summoned to the Minister's office. I could see straight away that he was not to blame for what had happened. He seemed at a loss himself; his little blue eyes had an expression of total confusion. For the first time he spoke to me without any official stiffness, as though I were a friend rather than a subordinate. Avoiding any hints about the reason for recent events, he asked me to take over a major portion of the Programme director's responsibilities and duties. He said he was sure I would be much better at dealing with the complex business of shaping policy in the field of film production than an outsider who was soon due to replace the previous director. He, the Minister, would be happy to back me any time I needed it. 'We must help each other in these unpredictable times, comrade,' he said, looking at me with anxiety and hope.

Three days later I was dancing at an exciting New Year's Eve party given by some close friends. My heart still throbbed with compassion for the injured man and silently rebelled against the injustice done to him. Yet, as the hours passed my sorrow gradually melted away in the atmosphere of exuberant joy. Despite the severe frost outside, it was hot in the room, the Christmas tree glowed with coloured lights, the little flat swarmed with people I knew and liked. The kitchen table was laid with good food brought by all the guests, an abundance of alcohol contributed to our merriment. Paul Anka, Eartha Kitt and Harry Belafonte, whose records we had brought from London, filled the place with their haunting voices. I danced deliriously, moving from one partner to another, ravishing in my Locarno silks, listening to whispered words of admiration. From time to time I caught anxious glances from Konrad and felt infinitely happy: a new chapter in my life was about to open, a chance to prove that

I could equal him. Then the clock announced the end of the old year, the lights went off, and we all kissed in the darkness. I was warm, I was radiant, I could hardly wait to see the new year and face my new challenges.

· 11 ·

Saturdays are for country walks. We set off at dawn and after a
few miles drive, leave our car behind and go off into the wild. The
open space welcomes us to the rising day, the freshening breeze,
the morning dew. We plunge into the deep silence broken only by
birdsong and the peaceful bleating of sheep. Walking fast –
Konrad first, alert, his camera ready, me far behind and deep in
my thoughts – we talk very little, but we are together. As we
stride alongside fields and plod across meadows, sinking from
time to time into a shadowy wood to re-emerge again in open
country, the shifting view unwinds before our eyes. The day is
reaching its peak. Great silence still prevails and we share it with
no one, though traces of human thought and toil are all about us.
We pass walls of dark Yorkshire stone, laid skilfully without
mortar, that after hundreds of years are still holding fast and
forming a patchwork design on this fertile land. The walls and
fences we pass, the gates we open and close, and the stiles we
climb, all speak of the days of the enclosures when 'sheep ate
people' at this very place. Sometimes our path takes us to a
graveyard of past industrial glory. The forlorn shells of once
powerful workshops bewail their fate with paneless windows,
with rust, weeds and decay. Drowsily flows the turbid current of
the Leeds-Liverpool canal dreaming of its bygone powers. An
abandoned railway track still runs – to nowhere. We walk in
silence, lost in mournful thoughts.

I knew nothing about this land when, many years ago, I learned we were going to live here. I opened an encyclopaedia and read that Leeds was 'a city in Yorkshire known mainly for its industries: engineering and electrical trades, paper and printing, textiles and metal goods'. What would I do amongst textiles and metal goods? The image of a dreary town coated with soot, puffing black smoke from its factory chimneys, haunted my sleepless nights. This image vanished as soon as we arrived. The breathtaking beauty of our new surroundings soothed my anxiety and became my consolation. Nonetheless, there was still nothing for me to do in this beautiful country.

Working with film scripts is a strange profession. You cannot take it with you to another country. To do this work well you have to be born into the country where the writing is done, into its language, history and literature. When I left Poland I knew that my professional life was at an end. But a life without work was for me out of the question. We could manage on Konrad's salary, but I was determined to learn a new skill and get a job. I needed to prove that I could still be useful away from my country; that my work was worth not only Polish zloties but also British pounds; that I was still flexible enough in my forties to find my own place in an alien society. Konrad had never asked that I prove myself in this way, but I wanted to show him that I could. I craved my daughters' recognition. And I needed my own self-respect.

I had to start from scratch mastering the language. I was reluctant to take a course or go to a private tutor – I wanted to learn in my own way. Twice a week I would sneak into a huge university lecture hall and, sitting there among young students, listen to lectures on English literature. At first it was hard to understand. But I soon got used to the teacher's pronunciation and started taking notes. Then at home, during my long hours alone, when the house was clean and the dinner cooked, I pored over the books that had been recommended, reading classics one after another and looking up any words I did not know. After a year of this work my knowledge of English would have been good enough to write a major dissertation on Tobias Smollett or Thomas Peacock, neither of whom I had ever heard of before, but was still not sufficient to talk about daily matters. As I was alone for most of the day, I had no one to talk to in any language. And it was no good trying to talk English at home in the evenings – we meant to, but always slipped back into Polish. I was often mocked by my daughters – they split their sides with laughter when I asked them for a 'shit of paper'. Aware of the dangers, I also preferred to remain silent when we were invited out, as we often were. It was a vicious circle. I finally resorted to an advanced Cambridge course – this procured me a certificate but I was just as terrified to open my mouth. I knew I would only start speaking if I went out and began work. It was time to look for a new skill.

The post-graduate course in librarianship at Leeds Polytechnic was very demanding and required extremely concentrated work. Students had to learn a great deal of new information in a very short time, and also acquire a whole new set of practical skills. For ten hectic months I sat at a school desk along with thirty other students who could have been my daughters or sons, who were born in this country and had only recently graduated from British universities. I felt a complete outsider and did my work in silence. When in June the finals came, I failed three out of nine exams and thus my diploma. There was no way of re-sitting the exams, I could only repeat the whole course. To this I said no. I could not face another year at a school desk. Come what may, even without formal qualifications, I would find myself a job.

*

The window of my new office overlooked the solemn statue of Adam Mickiewicz, the greatest of all Polish poets, and Krakowskie Przedmieście, one of the oldest and most charming streets of Warsaw. The Film headquarters had recently moved there from Puławska Street and was now housed in an old residential building, next to the Ministry of Culture and Art. The spirit of the good old days still hung over Krakowskie

Przedmieście, and seemed to penetrate right through the thick walls of the building into my room. Some pictures that I brought from home and some fresh flowers placed in an antique vase to brighten a dark corner, gave my room an air of comfort and elegance quite unlike that of any other office. My clients would admire the place whenever they entered: its pleasant atmosphere helped them feel at ease in discussing their scripts.

The staff of the new unit I had been put in charge of – two editors and a secretary – worked in an adjacent room. We got on quite well, though we were a motley bunch. One of the editors, Izabella, was a tall, stout woman nearing her fifties. She was an established writer with a rich literary output. Or rather she had been. She came from an old aristocratic family but had dissociated herself from them early in life because of her Communist convictions. After Stalin's death she went through a severe personal crisis, took to drink and stopped writing. Since the Party still cared for their stray sheep, they had sent Izabella to work in the new unit in the hope that doing something useful in good company might help her recover.

Ryszard, the second editor, was a young man straight from university where he had studied Polish literature. As happened every so often in our socialist country, the first job he was given in the film headquarters had little to do with his background. I discovered him poring in desperation over some statistic and pointed out to those responsible that he would fit much better in the script department. So to his great surprise and delight, he was promptly transferred to work with me.

The third member of the staff was Beata, now our secretary. When the old Programme director was dismissed, she refused to stay with his successor. She wanted to work with me and was immediately accepted. Her life had changed a great deal since we had last worked together in the educational department. Now she never looked hungry, she wore elegant clothes and smiled confidently at her colleagues. After her mother's death she remained single and lived comfortably enough on her own. The sinister time of Stalinist repression was long over. However, she was still looked askance at by less tolerant Party members, if not for her political past, at least for her deep Christian beliefs that she boldly proclaimed. She was the only one in our little unit who did not belong to the Party.

Our task, in this oddly matched little team, was to move Polish feature film production in a desirable direction. Reviewing film scripts submitted by producers was only one part of our work. Our main job was to look for new literary sources for film. This meant reading all new fiction, keeping in touch with publishing houses, authors and journalists. A newspaper report, a short story, an unpublished novel that dealt with topical themes, all these might be a source of future film scripts. We needed films showing contemporary life in Poland with all its intricacies and conflicts, all its achievements and failures. Having more than once singed their fingers on topical subjects, script writers and film directors tended to shun anything remotely related to problems of the day, and had retreated to literary classics and historical themes.

My new duties often kept me away from my cosy office. I had to attend many private screenings, take part in high-level meetings on general film policy, sometimes give a press or radio interview. The Minister rarely expressed any views at a conference without first consulting me. He took me along to any meeting that was to determine the fate of an important script or newly finished film. The new Programme director, formally my boss, did not interfere. Soon after he arrived, he came to my office to pay his respects and to offer his help should I need it. But there was no such need: he was not someone I would ever take seriously. He was a failed actor and had only been given this responsible job through someone's influence. He knew nothing about films or programming and was not even keen to learn. He respected my long experience, and seeing me as 'the Minister's person', tried hard to be nice.

My three subordinates were also nice to me, though sometimes this was embarrassing. Ryszard, for example, treated me like a sovereign, he showered me with blandishments and was for ever trying to attend to my well-being. Once he got hold of a huge directorial arm-chair and triumphantly dragged it up to my office.

It was difficult to explain that I didn't need an arm-chair to build up my prestige, and to persuade him to take the dreadful thing back.

Izabella, when sober, worked in silence, withdrawn and enigmatic. But more often than not she was drunk from early morning on. On such days a heap of unread scripts would pile up on her desk as she sat chattering away. Even then she was reluctant to talk about herself but would ask me endless personal questions as though she were considering me as a character for her next novel. But behind her keen professional interest of a writer I thought I could detect something else: a deep devotion, if not a kind of love. I was fond of her too, and pitied her terribly: stocky, untidy, her face always crimson, her closely cropped hair going grey, she must have felt unloved and very lonely.

Beata was the only person in my office I felt at ease with, although I knew she strongly disapproved of my Party membership. She was very frank and wished me well so she never refrained from telling me what she thought in her tactful, inoffensive way. Sometimes we argued, finally coming to the conclusion that my faith was as good as hers. But I was never sure that she was truly convinced of this.

Once I became the head of the new unit, I was no longer bothered with special Party assignments. I almost stopped going to the Party meetings too, because there was always something else important that I had to go to. To be honest, I was extremely pleased when, with a clear conscience, I could miss these dreadful assemblies. No one could accuse me of neglecting my Party work since everything I did was in the name of the Party and on behalf of its policies.

With this new appointment my salary doubled. I also earned a good deal of extra money from articles and interviews or being on the jury for all sorts of scriptwriting competitions. We were becoming rich, Konrad and I, to the extent that working people could become rich in Poland in the sixties. Little by little and imperceptibly, we were joining the ranks of the red bourgeoisie.

When his professor left on a foreign assignment, Konrad was given his chair. This contributed to our fortunes but also caused many worries. A lot of water had passed under the Warsaw bridges since the October turning point. Little of what we had hoped for from Gomułka, when we stood and cheered him in the huge square, had actually materialised. The love we all offered him went unrequited. It soon became clear that Gomułka was not the great reformer he had been hailed as. Little by little Party policy fell back into its old tracks. Many of those who had fought for change in 1956 were now accused of revisionist, anti-Marxist views. Some were purged from the Party, others were looked on askance and threatened with punishment unless they constrained their zeal. Any writers, scholars or students who claimed that the Stalinist legacy was still deeply rooted in our society were denounced as aides to the capitalist West, vilified and harassed. Censorship regained its former power and poked its nose into every printed work and screened picture. Internal security was reinforced – its mighty tentacles were again reaching far and wide.

Konrad was popular with his students, surrounded by followers and worshipped by his assistants. A large number of committed young people joined our circle of friends. However, Konrad was now branded as one of the most active revisionists and fell into disgrace with the Party bosses. As time went by he felt the effects of this more and more deeply. His books and articles were censored, his public statements condemned by official spokesmen, his behaviour closely watched. A dark cloud hovered over our busy life, thickening all the time.

A cloud also hung over my daily work. I frequently had to explain to a disappointed author that, although I greatly admired his script, there was no chance of it being approved by my superiors. Sometimes the exasperated writer or film director would make his way to the Minister, only to hear the same answer. Sighing, the Minister would raise his blurred little eyes and point at the ceiling: it was not *his* decision. At stormy meetings between top film producers and top Party representatives, the matter would be discussed again, and again a high-ranking Party official would raise his eyes to the ceiling, hinting it was not *him* but *them*. A sinister other-worldly force seemed to be taking decisions out of all mortal hands.

By that time Konrad had become known as a scholar and author well beyond the Polish border. His books and articles were published abroad. He received regular invitations to lecture or give papers at Western universities and international conferences. Permission to go and a passport often arrived only on the very last day before he was due to travel. Other times permission was refused and Konrad had to apologise to his foreign hosts. In the winter of 1966, after a year of suspense, he suddenly got leave to go to Manchester to take up a visiting fellowship for a few months.

This time our parting was not so hard for me to bear as it had been nine years before. I was overwhelmed by work – designing a course and editing a text-book for scriptwriters. Everything at home was going smoothly. The girls were busy at school, surrounded by friends, almost independent. They were very good company for me after a long, hard day at work. Lena had grown into a thoughtful, all but grown-up person and was a true friend. I could talk with her about anything that mattered, all the way from books and films to the upbringing of her young sisters. The twins still caused many problems, each one in her own way, but they were good company too. Though poles apart in character and quite different in appearance, habits and behaviour, they were both nonetheless equally tender and loving to me. They tried to cheer me up, telling me stories from school with a true satirical flair and aping their teachers till my eyes filled with tears of laughter. Like their father, they brought me little presents and flowers. I would find these surprise presents on my pillow when I finally went heavy-eyed to bed. But I desperately missed Konrad and even my daughters' closeness didn't fully make up for his absence. In May, when his time in Manchester came to an end and my special assignment was successfully completed, I left the household in Lena's care and, promised by friends they would keep an eye on the children, I flew to Paris. There, after many months of being apart, we finally saw each other again, at Le Bourget airport.

My life with Konrad has always been full of surprises, of unexpected joys following our difficult times, of profound happiness in the wake of sorrow. He has a rare gift for turning gloom into brightness, for making small misfortunes into an occasion for happiness never to be forgotten. Even a loathsome visit to the dentist becomes a pleasant affair when preceded by a long walk with him and followed by a cosy chat in an old pub. The most agonising times of our life together – the despair that he sometimes caused me, the times when we had to leave everything we loved and cherished and start a new life again, a first time, a second time – all these bitter days and years still sparkled with his radiant presence, warmed with his tenderness.

Those spring days in Paris shine in my memory like a dazzling light that casts into shade all the miseries of earlier and later times. We were young again, we were free, we were together. Paris offered up its beauty like a huge table spread with delicacies for the starving. A thrilling day imperceptibly grew into an intoxicating night and then there was a day again.

After a week of such frenzy we embarked on a long journey. Taking turns at the wheel of our new Cortina, which Konrad had bought in Manchester and collected in Paris, we drove south along the Loire, calling at all the ancient castles perched on its banks; to the picturesque Carcassonne, to Arles, to the Riviera. Then we plunged into the fading beauty of the Italian Renaissance: Tortona, Piacenza, Cremona . . . the very sound of those names brings back to me time-worn piazzas and narrow streets slumbering away the peaceful afternoon in torrid heat. In Verona we paid our respects to Juliet, swearing at her grave our own everlasting love. Venice was next and there we stopped to rest.

Our way back led through Yugoslavia, Austria and lovely old Prague. After five weeks of unalloyed bliss we were going home, hoping for the best.

*

Abandon all hope, all ye who at the age of 48, with no proper qualifications and broken English, enter the world of job-hunting. I repeated this to myself constantly as day after day I visited job centres and employment agencies. At night I pored over long columns of job vacancies advertised in the local newspapers. At first I looked only for library work – with all the information I had gathered over the last year I could surely cope. But there were very few vacancies in local libraries and the applications I sent in were all promptly turned down. So, very soon, I began to look at adverts for far less appealing jobs. They were there in abundance: bookshop assistants, typists and junior clerks seemed to be in special demand. Exploring these possibilities became a full-time occupation. My house turned into a small office. I wrote scores of letters, filled in dozens of application forms, composed long, impressive c.v.s. Most of the replies that dropped daily through the letter box contained nothing but disappointment, but I was sometimes invited to an interview. I attended all these, every time with a new flicker of hope. Alas, they always ended with the same formula – so sorry, the job has gone, we wish you luck elsewhere. After I had been refused the post of junior accountant in a small textile factory, and one as a secretarial aide at the local water authority, as well as two or three typing jobs in big offices in the city, I began to suspect that neither my age nor my foreign origins were the main reason for my failures. At the interviews I went to, the efficient young managers looked rather bewildered when I spoke about my past work experience and educational background: they clearly hated the idea of working with an over-qualified employee. So I changed my tactics, cleaned my c.v. of any university degrees or impressive past employment, and – hoping against hope – went on with my trials.

Just at this time the twins left home and settled in universities far away from Leeds. Deep silence replaced their brisk steps and bright voices; the cheerful crowd of young people lolling about in our ground floor rooms disappeared. The house grew big and gloomy.

My mother arrived from Israel, not yet sure whether to stay for good. She was in her early seventies and still physically fit, but she had never recovered from her grief over Sophie's death and was getting old and wasted. She longed for her younger grand-children whom she had left behind and seeing them again became the main purpose of her dwindling life. Day after day she spent long hours wandering to and fro in our quiet suburb. Sometimes, depressed by my repeated disappointments, I left my application forms and joined her for a mournful walk. Near to our home is a vast cemetery that looks like a flowery park. We often went there to brood and remember. And it was to this quiet place, a few years later, that she made her final journey to rest in eternal peace.

*

My mother was still strong and vigorous when, in the spring of 1967, she flew from Israel to see us in Warsaw. It was her first visit after leaving Poland eight years earlier. She was particularly lucky to get a visa – people who went to Israel in the fifties were not welcome back, even for a short stay, and were usually refused entry. But we did everything we could to get an exemption for her and finally succeeded. So here she was, joyful and tearful at the same time, looking forward to seeing all the people she had longed for and all the places she had always loved. Our flat became a centre for happy reunions. Relatives and Mother's old friends and colleagues crowded into our little rooms, drinking tea and talking. Or they took her out for nostalgic trips and parties. She thrived in this bustle, anxious to make the most of her six weeks' stay.

It was a happy time for all of us until news of a serious crisis in the Middle East suddenly shattered our peace of mind. All her joy gone, Mother stopped seeing people and stayed glued to the radio listening for news. The suspense grew hourly. When on the 5 June the Arab-Israeli war finally broke out, people all over the country tuned in to the BBC: it was hard to tell from the Polish news bulletins what was really going on, since from the very beginning of the war official propaganda condemned the Israelis as aggressors and reported the war only selectively – to prove their point rather than to inform. In defiance of the official line, many ordinary Poles responded to the first victories of the little state with an outburst of sympathy and pride. A taxi driver's witty remark – 'Our brave Polish Jews are giving hard times to those rotten Russian Arabs' – sped round Warsaw by word of mouth and fast became a watchword. Excitement was widespread. Jews and non-Jews followed the bulletins with bated breath. Friends and acquaintances kept phoning Mother to cheer her up and say they hoped for an Israeli victory.

As, from day to day, the odds appeared to be more and more in Israel's favour, the official campaign against 'the aggressors' gained increasing strength. Not only were those who actually fought in the remote country viciously attacked, but also, and above all, their supporters all over the world: namely, the 'Zionists'. Who these Zionists were supposed to be was not quite clear, but the subtleties were soon pushed aside and it became evident that 'Zionists' meant 'Jews', whatever their view of Israeli policies. Party organisations in factories and offices all over the country called mass meetings and passed resolutions, always unanimously, condemning Israel and her supporters. Everyone was supposed to sign these resolutions but employees of Jewish origin were singled out and pressed to do so with particular zeal.

The day after the Polish government broke off diplomatic relations with Israel, Mother begged us to take her to the Israeli embassy. She felt lost and wanted to ask whether she should leave Poland at once or could stay a little longer until her visa expired. So, feeling very anxious and upset, Konrad and I drove her to the embassy that Sunday morning.

Although Sunday was a working day at the embassy, the building seemed deserted. We wandered for a while from one empty room to another until in a messy office we finally came across some clerks busily packing piles of documents. There was little they could do to help as they were as confused as us and in great haste. But they cheered Mother up, saying that as far as they knew, nobody had been killed or wounded in Ramat Gan, the town where Sophie and her family lived. There was nothing more we could do in the embassy, so we left at once and drove to a café to help Mother relax.

When we had finished our cakes and coffee and were returning to the car, we were suddenly stopped by two strangers. They said they were police agents and asked to see our identification cards. Outraged, we asked to see their documents first and demanded the reason for their request. They obediently showed us their licences but refused to explain what was wrong. They gazed for a while at Mother's Israeli passport, wrote down all her and our details, then politely said goodbye and let us go.

Soon after our trip to the embassy Mother left, well before the expiry date of her visa. The Six-Day War was over and no one wanted her to leave but she no longer felt at ease: the raging anti-Zionist campaign distressed her. We parted in tears, not knowing whether we would ever see each other again.

Immediately after Mother's departure, a young relative was suddenly sacked. My mother was his only aunt whom he loved very dearly and had often called during the first few weeks of her stay. He was a lawyer and worked for the police as an expert on economic fraud. The day Mother left he was summoned to his boss and ordered to quit at once. The only reason given for this sudden dismissal was that he had been meeting a citizen of an enemy state.

The atmosphere of mistrust and prejudice rapidly thickened around us. On 19 June, speaking at the Trade Unions Congress, Gomułka made his own attitudes clear, calling Polish Jews 'citizens of two fatherlands' and comparing them to the Fifth Column – the Nazi agents in pre-war Poland. We felt suddenly unable to breathe freely.

Outwardly, however, nothing much changed in our daily life. Neither Konrad nor I were asked to sign the anti-Zionist declaration. We worked as usual, went on with our ordinary routine, enjoyed our evenings with friends.

Once, some time in July, one of our best friends unexpectedly turned up in my office. Pale and shaky, she whispered that she must talk to me in private. She would not speak in my office, so I left a half-finished script and hurriedly went out with her. In a little café, almost deserted at this time of day, she asked me to swear that I would never tell anyone but Konrad, not even her own husband, about her visit or about the message she was bringing me. I swore. Her husband, she began, her hands trembling, her eyes filling with tears, had last night met an old friend of his who was now a high-ranking Party official. This man had warned her husband against keeping in touch with us. He told him we had visited the Israeli embassy to congratulate them on their victory and, to prove this accusation, had shown him some photographs in which Mother, Konrad and I could be clearly seen leaving the embassy building.

As she talked, biting her fingernails and casting nervous, furtive glances about her, I felt a long-forgotten sense of menace creep into my heart. But I quickly pulled myself together: my friend needed comforting more than me. I tried to play the whole wretched matter down and jokingly said that I didn't expect her or her husband, both of whom had been best friends of ours for ages, to stop being our best friends or to suspect we might be Israeli spies. At this point my friend broke down and burst into tears. She spoke no more and we parted.

I told Konrad about this strange visit and for some time we both expected repercussions at work: it seemed unlikely that our respective bosses and Party organisations would not have been briefed about our alleged misbehaviour. But time passed and nothing happened. My Programme director called on me as ever to display his friendly feelings, the Minister could hardly live a day without asking my opinion, and most of our friends were still very keen to see us.

Living a busy life, surrounded by people all day long, we never felt the need to be particularly friendly with our numerous neighbours. A polite 'hallo' on the staircase or a casual word in the lift were good enough for us and for them. One neighbour, however, made no bones about his hatred of us. He was a police major and lived with his family immediately below our flat. He often knocked on his ceiling and woke us up in the middle of the night, shouting that we were making a terrible noise and disturbing his rest. Or he would complain of a leak that had allegedly ruined his flat because of our carelessness. Since both the leaks and the noise were pure imagination, we assumed he was mentally disturbed and tried not to worry. But we now ceased to feel free at home and had to watch our every move carefully, wearing soft slippers, hushing our children and visitors, and limiting our use of tap water.

The twins, by then eleven, were often at home alone since they came back from school well before Lena who was at the university till late. Once they let in two men who said they were plumbers and had come to repair the pipes that were leaking into the flat below. The girls were rather amused by this visit knowing well that there were no leaks and wondering why the plumbers, supposedly interested in the pipes, were so keen to examine the balcony, where they spent a long time. Another time two more strangers came to repair our telephone, though it was in perfect order. The girls let them in and then watched them dismantle the receiver and put it back together. We suspected our flat had been bugged but we had nothing to hide so were not too bothered.

In November that year I was once again sent abroad to represent Polish Film. This took me by complete surprise. With the poisonous air of anti-Jewish propaganda all around, I was certain my superiors no longer trusted me. But I must still have been considered trustworthy to have been asked to head a group of twelve experts going to exchange experiences with Hungarian film makers.

Six years had passed since my Locarno venture and this time I was less afraid of failing in my mission. I set off on the new adventure with great enthusiasm. And perhaps thanks to this enthusiasm, I remember this three-week official trip as one continuous success.

*

I must have looked enthusiastic during my interview for the job of school librarian. The headmaster, a thin, middle-aged man with a tiny moustache, showed us — three candidates shortlisted out of forty-five applicants — around the school premises. It was a large comprehensive school built in the late sixties on the remote outskirts of Leeds – a daring educational experiment by the Labour council. A recent fire had badly damaged the unusually rich library – the headmaster's special pride – built up with love and care to serve 1,500 pupils during the day and the local community in the evenings. The re-building of the library was under way; 15,000 books bought with the insurance money were temporarily stored in a hut. I could not conceal my rapture when we entered this little building tightly packed with boxes full of marvellous, brand-new books. They all had to be classified and catalogued before they could be shelved in the new library. This was the job awaiting the successful candidate. I prayed it would be me, but there was little hope: the other two women were relatively young, both English and with considerable experience of library work.

After the proper interview – half-an-hour's talk with the headmaster, his deputy and the young librarian who desperately needed help – I sat with the other two candidates in an empty classroom drinking tea and waiting for the result. While the other two chatted quietly, both of them hopeful of getting the job, I sat silent and withdrawn thinking gloomily about the empty days ahead and the scores of future vacancies I would have to apply for. Then the thin figure of the headmaster appeared in the doorway and, in a brisk manner that revealed his origins as an ex-officer in the Army, he announced my victory.

The five years that followed this first success in my foster homeland and my new humble career, were hectic almost beyond my strength and, despite the shrunken field of my work, more rewarding than anything I had done before. Every morning I travelled ten miles and walked two more to reach the distant school. At dusk I returned exhausted, not fit for any work at home. A hundred books had to be classified and catalogued every day. At the same time pupils had to be attended to, more and more often as the stock of books ready to be used gradually increased. Having to answer their queries made me terribly nervous at first. Most of the youngsters spoke a broad Yorkshire that I could hardly understand; they all used a school slang totally obscure to me; some were very backward and found it hard to explain what they needed. But I had to help them find the right book, give the proper information, show them how to look up a word in a dictionary or encyclopaedia. I constantly made disgraceful mistakes. I would produce a beautiful album of Old Masters when, stammering and dropping her H's, a third-form girl had asked for a book on horses – to me it sounded like 'artists'. Or I gave a six-former information on airports when for his project he had asked for data on imports. Luckily the children understood me better, though they would often burst into laughter when I spoke: they had never met a foreigner before. I was not offended and laughed heartily with them, realising how funny I must sound. The kids seemed to like me for that. Very soon I got used to their way of speaking and made fewer blunders.

My boss, the librarian, who shared all the work with me, was a twenty-three-year old girl. She had great respect for me and I for her. She was competent, efficient and totally devoted to her work. After a few months, when the new library was finally rebuilt, all the books catalogued, put into their dust-jackets and displayed on the shelves, we split the work between us: she stayed in the back room to deal with all financial and administrative tasks, and I was put in charge of the library itself, acting mainly as reader's adviser.

This was challenging work. As early each morning I entered the library, still quiet and smelling of fresh paint, my heart filled with infinite joy and pride. Here was I, a newcomer in this foreign land, taking charge of these long rows of shelves containing thousands of beautifully published books waiting to be read by scores of young Britons. Here was I – at home between these walls because I had worked so hard to turn the piles of odd volumes into a library. Here was I, awaiting my readers and ready to give them my time, my skills, my knowledge. Through the huge library windows I could see crowds of pupils surging into the vast playground and making their way to school: another long day was about to begin. Terror would suddenly grip me by the throat: would I be able to manage? But I did. Day after day, term after term, year after year. There were some small failures –

sometimes I could not stop pupils from making a noise and then got sour words from the headmaster; but also small successes – when the right book, information or picture found its way to a grateful reader. The library was always full and my help in constant demand, from pupils as well as from teachers. Once a week I stayed on into the evening to serve the local community: old ladies looking for books on knitting and flower arranging; young mothers in search of romances and books on child care; newly retired people wanting to find out about hobbies or satisfy their life-long thirst for knowledge.

As time passed, I got to know my young customers better, and not only as readers. I heard about their joys and worries, their hopes and dreams. I knew now that very many of those children lacked parental care and looked somewhere else for love. A word of praise, a friendly touch, a sign of warm concern made them relaxed and happy. In trying to give them all this, I little by little acquired qualities I had never possessed before: patience and understanding.

*

After three weeks of intense work, interspersed with marvellous parties thrown by our hospitable Hungarian hosts, I returned from Budapest to Warsaw. Konrad was waiting for me at the Okęcie airport. I could see at first glance that something was wrong – he looked downcast and nervous. For a long while we could not speak in private: the eleven experts in the delegation were keen to meet him and say how proud he should be of his wife. Only when we had retreated to the car and set off on our way home, did I hear the alarming story.

During my stay abroad, Lena had celebrated her eighteenth birthday. That afternoon she had invited some of her friends home and for several hours they had all sat quietly in her room discussing books they had recently read – this was their favourite pastime. When at about eleven the young people left our flat and were making their way downstairs, they were suddenly stopped by the police major and accused of being a gang of hooligans.

A police van was waiting at the entrance and the major, brandishing a gun, forced the bewildered students inside. Lena, who was standing on the balcony to wave goodbye to her friends, saw all this happen and raised the alarm. Konrad immediately jumped in his car and went off in search of the young people. He soon found them at the Warsaw police headquarters, taken there for interrogation. Calling from a public telephone he quickly rang up the parents of the young people involved and two of the fathers hastened to their rescue. They happened to be prominent men and members of the Party. They testified on behalf of the whole group and the enraged major had to give up and let the students go. The whole incident took no more than an hour, but it shattered our last illusion of 'normal' life.

We were besieged. At work I basked in the glory of my recent success, but at night fear crept out from the dark corners of my bedroom and kept me awake.

Christmas that year was dismal, swollen with anxiety. On Boxing Day, without previous arrangement, two couples we knew turned up at our flat. Throughout our married life Konrad and I had befriended all sorts of people, young and old. Some of them were Jews, some not, it wasn't important either way. This time, however, with the exception of one of the wives, we were all Jews and for once it mattered: the same anxiety had brought us all together. Our visitors were in their fifties and all had many years of political involvement behind them. Before the war they had belonged to the communist movement and had been punished with prison sentences. In post-war Poland they had continued to serve the communist cause and had been rewarded with influential posts. Now, all of a sudden, their whole lives' work was in question. The younger man had been sacked from his job, the older one forced to take early retirement. At stormy meetings in their respective offices they had been accused of Zionism and expelled from the Party. And so was one of the women. They sat in our living room, smoking, drinking and pondering miserably over recent events.

'I have fought against Zionism all my life,' said the younger man. 'And I will strongly condemn what Dayan is doing now. Why me?' 'And why me?' shrugged the older man. 'In my *shtetl* before the war there were only two kinds of Jews: Zionists and communists. They always argued with each other. A gang of boys in my street, including me, used to attack the Zionist boys in the next street to teach them a lesson. I fought against them with my fists, then with my tongue and pen. Why me?'

Konrad sat silent, his head in his hands, his face showing signs of sleepless nights. I looked at him in agony. Was it not him who had shattered my Zionist daydreams and set me on the path to communism? Was it not him who now passionately condemned Israel for insisting on keeping the Arab lands after the Six-Day War? Why him?

The wife of the younger man then said that she was being harassed at work for being a Zionist, although she was not even Jewish. During the Nazi occupation she had risked her life to save a Jewish family by hiding them under her roof. And now, thirty-odd years later, in her own country that called itself Socialist, she felt threatened again for being close to Jews.

She talked nervously, wrenching her handkerchief. Memories of my own young years flooded into my mind and I felt my flesh creep: was another time of running and hiding about to begin?

'Let's call a spade a spade,' said the older man, trying to light a new cigarette from the butt of his last one. 'They've found a handy word to hide the ugly truth. They throw mud at Zionists, but what they really mean is Jews, Jews as a whole, anyone they can call a Jew just because his grandmother happened to be Jewish. Remember Adolf Hitler? We are entering a new era of anti-Semitism in this country . . .' 'For God's sake don't blame this country, don't blame the people,' I suddenly exclaimed, then blushed for having interrupted him. He seemed a little surprised. 'No,' he said, 'I don't blame the nation. This new anti-Semitism has been hand-made by the communist government which we helped to create ourselves, and fanned by the communist party to which we belonged . . .'

'And who desperately need a scapegoat to draw people's

attention away from soaring prices and from empty shelves in the butchers' shops,' chimed in his wife.

'That's true, but it isn't the whole truth,' said the other woman. 'People don't become anti-Semitic just because of queues in the shops. General Moczar* is after power, and he's trying to play on Polish nationalist feelings. The aliens, the Zionists are everywhere, he says, they have all the top jobs, they're betraying the country, swamping the Party. It's time to get rid of them and bring in true Polish patriots.'

'The kind of sloganeering is very catching,' said Konrad. 'Remember – there have been no major purges in the last few years. The paths to promotion are blocked, bosses are a few miserly years older than their deputies – look how long people have to wait to be rewarded for their hard work.'

'We should have known it would all end like this!' sighed the old man, lighting a new cigarette. 'But we were all comfortable in our cosy Party nest. We flew to it like moths to fire. We believed we did it for justice and equality. We refused to see warning lights, even though they were there from the beginning. The Kielce pogrom in 1946, the purges . . . We put up with it, we thanked our lucky stars that we personally were still untouched. We hoped we would escape for ever. Now it's time to pay the bill for our own blindness.'

'The evil is indivisible,' remarked Konrad vaguely. 'If you close your eyes when others are trampled on, you give up the right to a better fate.'

'If only we were younger and knew at least one foreign language between the two of us,' said the woman who was not Jewish. 'We would leave at once and start from scratch somewhere else.'

'Yes, it's too late for us, too,' sighed the older man. 'But fortunately providence has saved us from having children.' He gave Konrad and me a questioning glance.

---

* General Mieczysław Moczar – a war-time partisan leader, according to some, closely connected with Soviet security. In 1960s he made a bid for power getting support from a motley alliance of former combatants, left communists, nationalists and ever-growing groups of frustrated Party functionaries.

When our visitors left that night, we looked at each other without a word. We went to bed and lay silently in the darkness knowing that we both were thinking the same thing. But all these thoughts were gone by the next morning: neither of us could seriously think of living away from Poland.

*

Christmas Eve descends from the darkening sky and paints the windowpanes with a dense greyness. The postman drops the last Christmas cards through our letterbox and vanishes behind the hedge. From next door comes the sweet tune of a well-remembered carol and fills the room with peace. Memories of a distant childhood come back with the warm scent of vanilla and yeast. The house grows solemn with expectation.

Tomorrow in this room a tiny grandson will crawl on the soft carpet and warm our ageing hearts with his cheerful cooing. The twins will be here, nicely dressed and blooming, forgetting for a short time all their daily worries. And their English husbands will be happy too, delighted to share in our foreign customs. Old friends will make their weary way from London to join us at our festive table. The house will come to life again with quick steps and merry voices.

But now we sit at our dark window waiting for the first star, wrapped in memories. Far away, lights are shining on a winding road, forming a huge bow of brightness. Somewhere at the distant end of this luminous bow is the school where I once belonged and which after many years still holds perhaps a faint trace of my work and enthusiasm. Now this too is only a time to remember.

*

To celebrate the end of that momentous year of 1967 and to greet – with little hope – the coming of 1968, we were invited by another couple of friends to a late dinner party. Only ten people gathered round the table that night, some of us Jews. The mood was subdued. Conversation trickled reluctantly and nobody was keen to tell jokes or suggest dancing. Shortly before midnight our host switched on the television for a satirical programme. We had all been looking forward to it: programmes on New Year's Eve were always particularly good, written and performed by the best satirists and comedians. They were irreverent, often daring, as though the stiff, humourless face of the censor was looking the other way on that one special night. This time, however, the little screen breathed out sheer hatred. A hook-nosed puppet climbed up a huge globe, its arms widespread, its claws greedily clutching the surface. Small hook-nosed figures scattered around the globe pushed or pulled the big one up and up. At the same time an unfamiliar male voice sang out Dayan's song thanking his 'brothers-in-law from all countries in the world' for their help and support.

Our host stepped to the television and briskly switched it off. Too late. Four of us, Dayan's hook-nosed helpers, sat thunderstruck, profoundly shaken. The six remaining friends hung their straight noses down.

Parting from my Party card proved easier than I ever expected. Back at work after the New Year break, I asked the secretary of my organisation to come to my office for a private word. She was a woman I had never had much respect for and with whom I had little in common. I dreaded having to explain to her why I had decided to leave the Party. I had my card ready in my hand when she entered the room. Without inviting her to sit down, I handed it over to her and asked her to cross my name off the Party files. Her response took me by surprise: she burst into tears and kissed me wholeheartedly. Tucking the stiff booklet into the pocket of her cardigan, she left my office without a word.

On the same day, at the same time, Konrad went in search of his Party secretary at the still half-deserted university. He found him and handed in his card. The man did not seem much surprised.

· 12 ·

A powerful wave of discontent, the first for twelve years, swept Poland at the beginning of 1968 and grew daily more intense. Food shortages in the shops, overt or concealed price rises, the fast-widening gap between those who could afford expensive goods and those who could not, spelled trouble. Internal security was on full alert. And so were the censors.

On 30 January, on its thirteenth night, the classic Polish drama, *The Forefathers*, was taken off the stage at the National Theatre in Warsaw.

For more than a century this powerful work of romanticism by the national bard, Adam Mickiewicz, had inspired successive generations of Poles with patriotism and the love of freedom. During the time of Poland's partitions it sustained the free spirit of an enslaved nation and rallied it against its main oppressor, the Russian Tsar. It was often seen as the dream that came true in independent Poland between the two wars. It was read again like a biblical prophecy during the German occupation. The new production of this old but never ageing play was a major cultural event in Warsaw. It ran every night to full houses and provoked powerful responses in the audience. The lines condemning the Tsar and calling for freedom were repeatedly interrupted with loud applause. Some people on high obviously did not like it.

The decision to ban the play was leaked a few days before it was actually taken off the stage, so on 30 January the theatre was bursting with people who knew it was their last chance to see *The*

Forefathers. Konrad and I were sitting next to the aisle, jostled and pushed by people who had managed to get tickets at the very last moment and were standing or sitting on the floor in the aisle. There were lots of students in the audience next to well-known people from the artistic and literary world, but some of the rows were packed with blank-eyed men whose profession left nothing to the imagination. The words of the play seemed to take on a special relevance and were received as direct messages to the audience. Time and again loud shouts and bursts of applause interrupted the performance. More often than not, it was the blank-eyed men who shouted and applauded first. In their excitement the students hardly noticed who was leading them. At the final curtain the audience rose and the walls of the National Theatre resounded with an immense clamour of applause and protest. As if informed in advance of such an outcome, uniformed policemen stepped into the hall.

In the big square in front of the theatre, a group of students with banners protesting against the banning of the play was quietly waiting for the end of the performance. In the dark streets behind their backs police lorries were waiting, too. Thirty-five students were arrested that night and on the following day eight of them were singled out, accused of hooliganism and ordered to pay high fines. They were later suspended from the university. Most of the students selected for this exemplary punishment were Jewish.

Once launched, the wave of student protests spread quickly. Throughout February scores of demands were put into words, signed by thousands of students and sent off to the authorities or passed from hand to hand. They called for freedom of speech, they protested against censorship, against the secret police, against inequality in a socialist country. They also strongly condemned the blatant racism in official propaganda. As the unrest gathered strength, so did the repression. Students were arrested, expelled from the university, deprived of grants. A large number of academic staff, as well as those writers and artists who backed the student demands, were also threatened and harassed.

Forgetting his personal worries, Konrad went once more into

the unequal fight. Many of his students were being severely victimised and needed their tutors' help and guidance. This they were all given by Konrad and his co-workers, as well as by many other staff all over the univeristy.

In the meantime, my world remained strangely quiet. The response to my withdrawal from the Party was unexpectedly slow. I waited daily for the blow to fall and meanwhile said nothing to Party members about my decision, being pretty sure they knew already but preferred not to talk about it. The only person I spoke to was Beata. She was deeply moved when she heard I had left the Party. 'But why did you wait so long?' she asked. There was bitter reproach in her voice. For once I knew she was right.

At the beginning of the new year some new faces appeared in the film headquarters. One of the newcomers joined the Pro-gramme Department. He wore a military uniform. The Minister told me that the captain was interested in scripts and films about the war and the army. I should help him find what he needed. But the captain was very stand-offish when we met and curtly said he could manage on his own. Some time later I saw him talking to Ryszard and found out that many scripts were missing from my unit's archives. When I asked him about this Ryszard looked a bit embarrassed but admitted lending the typescripts to the captain. After that I stopped asking questions. Ryszard became almost unavailable, spending most of his time in a secluded little room that was now the captain's office.

Having lost one of my assistants, I was inundated with work. Izabella was little help. The ideological battle going on between the intellectuals and the authorities outside her office seemed only to whet her thirst. She sat at her desk drunk and idle all day long. Listening to her chaotic twaddle I realised she was totally confused, not knowing where to place her sympathies. She would look at me keenly straight in the eyes and warmly squeeze my hand cursing the anti-Semites, but five minutes later she would declare her full support for the Party and its policies. Beata would look at me and I at her. We were both very fond of Izabella and pitied her.

On the last day of February the Minister asked me to come to his office. The Programme director was summoned there too. They both looked a little solemn as I entered the room. Trying not to show any signs of anxiety, I sat down in one of the ministerial leather armchairs and braced myself to hear the verdict.

'Dear comrade,' began the Minister, and paused. The Programme director was closely inspecting an intricate design on the carpet. 'Dear comrade,' resumed the Minister, 'the Central Committee of our Party insist that we strengthen our efforts in the field of contemporary scriptwriting. They want us to build up a strong network of competent editors and writers fully committed to our cause. I would like you to help me in organising this large, important unit and then take charge of it. What do you think?'

I sat speechless, hardly believing my ears. He didn't know a thing, they had kept him in the dark. I glanced at the Programme director but his gaze was fixed on the stuccoes of the ceiling.

'I feel honoured, Minister,' I said at last, regaining my composure, 'but I don't think I'm the right person for the job. I can't possibly accept a Party assignment, since I'm no longer a Party member.'

'What?!' If a winged cow had suddenly flown into the Minister's office he could not have been more perplexed. His mouth open, his little eyes more blurred than ever, he stared at me in disbelief. 'Are you sure? Why? What has happened?' he mumbled. The shadow of a grin played vaguely on the thin lips of the director. I remained silent.

'Please, tell me comrade,' the Minister pulled himself together and assumed his usual fatherly way of addressing me. 'Is there something wrong with your children? Can you no longer combine your Party and family duties?' There was a flicker of hope in his voice.

'My children are fine, Minister,' I said. 'And my decision has nothing to do with my family life.'

'So, why? Why, for God's sake?'

I told him everything – all the reasons that I had explained to no one else so far. That I could not comply with the rules of a party that approved of police violence. That I strongly objected to belonging to an organisation that stifled freedom, perpetrated injustice and promoted racism in the country. That I had ceased to feel I could belong and therefore had to leave. The Minister listened in silence, the expression of puzzlement in his eyes giving way to one of deep sorrow.

On Friday 8 March I stood by my office window looking down at the street. Innumerable bunches of fresh flowers laid by unknown hands at Mickiewicz's feet formed a lake of colour and contrasted brilliantly against the dark statue and the cloudy sky. My desk was heaped with scripts waiting to be read but I couldn't start work. A rally in defence of democratic freedoms had been called for noon that day by students at the university courtyard. I knew that both Konrad and Lena would be there. I strained my eyes, trying to get a glimpse of the gathering crowd, but though the university was very near to my office, the winding street prevented me from seeing its gate. Large groups of students were hurrying along Krakowskie Przedmieście and gradually vanishing from sight.

I returned to my desk and tried to concentrate on reading but just before noon a heavy rumble in the street made me jump to my feet and run back to the window. Huge lorries covered with tarpaulins were making their way from the north to the south of the city. The tarpaulins were slightly raised at the back to let in air and I could see that the lorries were tightly packed with men in civilian clothes. A sudden wave of wartime memories brought back times when lorries like these, full of armed Nazis, had rumbled along the streets of Warsaw hunting for victims.

The sinister column slowly proceeded towards the university campus. Seized with terror, I grabbed the telephone and with a shaking hand dialled Konrad's office. There was no answer. It was twelve o'clock already and they must have all gone to the rally. Without thinking, and forgetting my coat, I ran down to the street and hurried to the campus. But it was too late: a police cordon had cut off the traffic and was ordering back all pedestrians.

Nobody in the office did any work that day. When I got back to my room, Beata and some of my colleagues from other departments joined me at the open window. Ryszard was absent without reason; Izabella was dozing at her desk in the next room.

The street was deserted and quiet, all the lorries gone. Only police patrols with truncheons ready at hand walked up and down the pavements. Suddenly we heard something: a gust of south wind brought a clamour of voices to our ears. Holding our breath we listened. Soon the faint sound of tangled shouts and screams gave way to a distinct murmur of chanting. We strained our ears. 'Gestapo! Gestapo!' chanted hundreds of voices, and then, 'Freedom! Freedom!'

What exactly happened that day at the university courtyard I learnt only that evening when, after braving unruly crowds of students chased through the main streets by police and their civilian helpers, I returned from work, and when Konrad and Lena together with some of her friends, finally managed to get home. Although the Rector had declared the rally illegal, about 1,500 students had gathered in the courtyard at noon. Two resolutions were read out and accepted with unanimous applause. One condemned the banning of *The Forefathers* as a violation of the Polish constitution; the other demanded acquittal of the indicted students. Though the atmosphere in the courtyard was heated and extremely tense, the meeting went smoothly and without any serious incidents until, all of a sudden, the ancient university freedom was violated by the heavies from the covered lorries who burst into the inner courtyard and began to beat up the students, men and women alike. The students started chanting 'Gestapo' and 'Freedom'. In the growing turmoil it soon became impossible to distinguish between victims and assailants. But then the leader of the rally ordered all the students to sit on the ground and immediately the picture became clear: there were about five hundred intruders in the courtyard. For the rest of the rally, the young people sat in the bitter cold on filthy heaps of melting snow. They sang the Polish anthem and the Internationale, waiting for the deputy Rector to appear. They left the courtyard only when they were granted an official meeting on the following

Monday. But then, when they left the campus, they were attacked with truncheons again and what had started as a peaceful meeting turned into an unequal battle which quickly spread all over Warsaw.

Perishing with cold from sitting on the snow for two hours, sneezing and coughing, Lena and her friends now tried to remember all the details of the afternoon. One boy's forehead was bruised, a girl's coat was torn – souvenirs of their brief encounters with the police and civilian agents. They had seen some of their colleagues being knocked down, beaten up and taken away. They were worried about various friends who should by now have turned up. Lena, glued to the telephone, was desperately trying to get in touch with someone who seemed to have vanished. I saw her crying in the dark corridor.

That night the radio and television reported that a group of hooligans had caused riots in Warsaw, attacking the police, shouting anti-Soviet slogans and disturbing public order.

The next day the papers reported the riots, just briefly, and claimed that all the leaders of the student unrest were Zionists and enemies of the Polish nation. The fight was gathering momentum. A rally was called at the Warsaw Polytechnic in support of the university. The students protested against the press, shouting such slogans as 'The Press lies' and 'There is no bread without freedom'. They marched along the streets waving national flags and singing patriotic as well as communist songs. This time the police used not only truncheons but also tear gas.

When I arrived at work on Monday, the windows in several of our offices were broken and a powerful smell of gas still hung in the building: a group of hunted students had tried to hide here the day before and had been seized by the police. The newspapers were now full of lurid descriptions of the riot leaders. Their names were printed, and also those of their parents, whose past and present lives and careers were described in detail. One major conclusion was drawn: they were all Jews in responsible jobs; they were all Zionists conspiring against Poland.

'Take a good look at these people. Is this who you really want to help undermine your own country?' Such were the calls in the press and the official leaflets distributed to young people everywhere.

The student protest spread rapidly all over the country, soon reaching most universities, polytechnics, colleges and even some of the high schools. The media repeated the same names over and over again, and it was not long before more were added to the black-list: those of the prominent writers and professors who were responsible for educating these young hooligans. On the fourth day Konrad's name along with those of many of his friends appeared in all the daily papers, to be viciously spat on by the radio and television. Some time later the Faculty of Philosophy and Social Sciences was closed without explanation, and all lectures and seminars were banned. The police made a close search of the premises and bugged the departmental rooms. However, Konrad and his colleagues still reported to work each morning and stayed in the Department all day long: the bewildered, harassed students needed their advice and support.

I too went to my office as usual but my desk was little by little becoming empty. The pile of scripts I had been working on since 8 March was gradually melting away and there were very few new ones coming in. My telephone almost never rang, and when it did it was a friend wanting to ask how I was. My clients rarely talked to me about their projects, the Programme director avoided my room and the Minister suddenly stopped needing my help. So, more and more often, I found myself with no work to do, though many of my colleagues and film producers still dropped in from time to time for a chat. Strangely enough, some of them had never been so friendly before.

Then, after several days of sinister silence, the internal mail brought me an official letter signed by the Minister. It said that as from that day I was dismissed from my post as head of the unit but that I should continue my work as an editor. There was no reason given, no legal paragraph quoted.

I sat at my desk staring blankly at the short message and waiting for a telephone call: I was sure that the Minister would ring me in a minute to say how sorry he was and to explain that in the circumstances there was nothing else he could do. But the telephone stayed silent, I was waiting in vain. On the same day, without waiting to be told, I collected all my belongings and moved to the next room, joining Beata and Izabella. Ryszard's desk was vacant, so I settled down there with my very last script.

The next morning the Programme director summoned the staff of my unit for a briefing. Beata was not invited, so apart from myself only Izabella and Ryszard, who had somehow managed to report at work after a long absence, took part in this meeting. The Programme director briefly informed my two colleagues in a very dry and formal manner of my dismissal and asked them to assess my past performance as their boss. Ryszard seemed to be just ready and waiting for such an opportunity. Avoiding my glance, he delivered a long and fluent speech in which he accused me of being greedy for work, of doing everything myself, of keeping my assistants in the dark and thus denying them any chance of sharing in the noble struggle for committed, socialist Polish films. I looked at him bewildered, hardly believing my ears. He had obviously learnt his lines well in advance. When he finally stopped, the director turned to Izabella: 'And what is your opinion, comrade?' Instinctively, I heaved a little sigh of relief: I knew that – sober or drunk – she would in a moment turn this preposterous accusation to ridicule. Izabella sat cool and aloof, her gaze wandering miles away. 'Yes,' she said, 'Ryszard is quite right.' She was sober.

On 19 March a mass meeting of Party activists from all over the country was held at the huge Congress Hall of the Palace of Culture and Science. It was broadcast live and we all, the whole family and a friend, sat down in front of the television to watch it from beginning to end. With just a faint hope in our hearts we waited impatiently for Gomułka to appear. Perhaps he would condemn the horrific behaviour of the police or put a brake on the wild outpourings of the media? Or perhaps just spell out some kind of rules in this dreadful game?

The tension in the tightly packed hall seemed to penetrate right into our own little room. There was something going on in the auditorium that we couldn't make out – hostile shouts could be heard from distant rows that were evidently shunned by the TV cameras.

At last Gomułka arrived, only to dash our last remaining hopes. He justified the banning of *The Forefathers*, calling the production an anti-Soviet provocation; he stated that the riots had been brought about by a bunch of students of Jewish origin; he accused the bankrupt politicos, such as some well-known writers and scholars, of conspiring against Poland. Here Konrad was mentioned, along with some of his friends.

The Communist Party leader then went on to talk about Zionism and Jews. As he spoke the audience – the most devoted Party members – roared out, 'More! More! Down with Zionists!' There were some people of Jewish origin, Gomułka explained, who saw themselves as Poles not first and foremost Jews, and even did valuable work for the country – these people were welcome to live and work with us. The audience obviously did not care much for this generosity. But they warmed up a little as he went on: there were other Jews who saw themselves as citizens of the world – these cosmopolitans could stay here if they liked but they should not be allowed to maintain positions of responsibility. Then came the climax of Gomułka's presentation, greeted by wild enthusiasm: there was also, he said, a third kind of Jew – the Zionists, people whose allegiance was with Israel rather than Poland. Such people should leave our country. 'At once! Now! Today!' roared the audience. 'They must first apply,' said Gomułka with a slight grin. There was uproar in the auditorium – howls, roars, the cries of 'Down with Zionists!' and 'Now! Today!' The assembly turned into a raging mob.

In our cosy room, in our peaceful home, we suddenly felt ourselves in mortal danger. The enraged rabble would soon leave the Congress Hall and pour out onto the streets. If they were sober now, they would not be so for long. We told our friend to leave. Her husband's name had not been mentioned, she would be safer at home. She slipped out immediately and went through the loft so that no one would see her coming down our stair-case that was certainly watched. Left on our own, Konrad, I and our three girls locked ourselves in the flat, blocked the front door with a heavy chest and looked for some sharp tools, just in case . . .

The night passed quietly, despite our fears – there was no violence in the streets, no pogrom. In the morning we left home as usual. Konrad and Lena went to the university, the twins hurried to school, and I reported to work. But we were scared.

Since the day of my dismissal I had received no mail at work and there was nothing left for me to do in the office. I spent long hours at my empty desk day after day pretending to read a book and trying not to look at Izabella who by now had sunk completely into drunken oblivion. I would gladly have resigned from work or at least applied for my annual holiday, but I couldn't do that: it had been tacitly agreed with other harassed friends, mainly those at the university, that we should cling to our work, resist all pressures to leave and never give in of our own free will – this would be playing into the hands of our persecutors. So I stayed there, cheered up all the time by Beata and many other colleagues. They did everything they could to help me put up with my long hours of enforced idleness. People I hadn't seen for ages, friends from the remote past, would turn up at my door to comfort me. One of them was Marek.

When Marek finished studying in 1956, our ways parted. He spent most of his time in Łódź making films, one after another. His most recent one had won an award at an international festival. He was making a brilliant and well-deserved career. Whenever we met, usually by chance, I would tease him, saying he was too big now to keep in touch with me. Marek would protest fiercely and explain that he had been terribly busy. But once he spoke his mind very openly. 'It's not me who has grown too big,' he said. 'It's you who have got too deeply involved in the establishment.' I was hurt at first but after a time I realised he might be right. I had always trusted his judgement.

Now, all these years later, he came to my office one day and took me out for a walk, since this was the only way of talking privately. He was terribly upset by what was going on, so much so that I felt it was him who needed comforting more than me. I said he had suffered enough in the past and deserved to live in peace without getting involved in things that had very little to do with him. It was my turn to suffer now, I said, and he should keep away from me, as there were eyes and ears all around and being seen in my company could be damaging to his work, and also to his family's hard-won peace. But Marek walked on next to me, silent and listless, as though he hadn't heard what I'd said. After a long silence he said at last: 'I don't ask for whom the bell tolls.' And he smiled shyly as though embarrassed at using big words.

After this first visit Marek called and took me out for a walk every other day. I felt safer in his company, and as we wandered along the familiar streets, sometimes in heavy rain, I could not help thinking about the war and of another brave friend who, heedless of his own safety, used to take me out from my hiding place for a breath of fresh air at times when it was least dangerous to do so – at dusk, in the mist or in the rain.

When my 'working' hours were over, I would walk to the university to meet Konrad and we would go home together. It was better for him not to be alone in the streets. Some of those mentioned in Gomułka's speech had been attacked. A prominent Catholic writer had been pulled into a dark gateway and beaten up by some ruffians. Someone else had been knocked down by a lorry on a pedestrian crossing. One day on my way to the university I saw a splendid car drawing up at the Ministry entrance. A man dressed in the dark suit of a high-ranking official got out of the car and our eyes met. Without thinking I smiled and was just about to greet him, when Wojtek Gruda – his gaze cool, his eyes blank, and his lips tight closed – turned round and walked away.

Early on 25 March, the radio announced the immediate dismissal of six professors from the University of Warsaw. Academic tenure and immunity, which had always been respected, even by the Russian Tsar, was now violated. An important new chapter was opening in the history of Polish universities.

So, Konrad suddenly found himself without work. That morning he stayed at home when I left for work. All I remember of that day is a small, moist bunch of violets dropped, as if by accident, on my empty desk by one of Poland's greatest writers; and the innumerable cups of strong black coffee brewed for me by the tireless Beata.

The names of the six professors, announced by the media as the most blatant examples of political misbehaviour, were reported over and over again. Very soon strong protests were made against their unlawful dismissal by Polish students and intellectuals, by colleagues in Czechoslovakia who were just then revelling in their short-lived freedom, and also in the West. The professors were not the only ones who suffered however – thousands of lesser known people were also being purged from the universities and publishing houses, from radio, film and theatre, and from the civil service. No one heard about them. Only a few people had the courage to speak up on their behalf. I heard from another friend about Marek's rage when he learned that two people in his studio were to be sacked without rhyme or reason. Quiet and self-effacing as he was, he went to a Party meeting at his studio and shouted that this was outrageous, hammering his fist on the table. Later, he slammed the door in an executive's face when all his efforts to defend the defenceless proved to no avail. No one else tried to help them.

On 1 April the Programme director told me I should apply at once for my annual holiday. I had no wish to stay at work but tried to argue against this, saying that I had planned my vacation for August so I could go to the sea with my children. But he said flatly I must go now – my clients and colleagues no longer trusted me and wanted me out. I knew this to be a lie but could not bring myself to insist on staying. I packed some of my belongings and feeling too hurt to say goodbye to anyone, immediately left the office.

We now entered a long period of disconcerting idleness. Only the twins hurried off to school in the morning. The rest of the family had no need to hurry. We forbade Lena to go to the university – further involvement in the students' cause would only help the propaganda. 'Like father, like son' was the slogan of the day, enthusiastically repeated by the media. Lena did not protest against our order, she knew we were right. Alternately excited and depressed, she spent most of her time with friends in the same predicament and who had not yet been arrested.

Konrad and I could now spend our days together as never before. But we were seldom alone. Day after day, from early morning till late at night, people flocked to our flat. Friends, acquaintances, Konrad's assistants and students, colleagues – his and mine – even strangers called on us constantly to discuss the latest news and rumours, to cheer us up or simply to show they did not run with the hounds. Now and again we were invited out to parties and dinners. Whenever we left the house and got into the car, another car, or sometimes two, would switch on their engines and closely follow us to our destination. When later we left, the same cars would still be waiting patiently in the dark and would shadow us back home. Our telephone was tapped and so was every nook and cranny of the flat. They always knew in advance when and where we were planning to go. But it did not stop people from giving their full names on the phone and saying what they thought. Some calls were hostile though. These were usually anonymous: a stranger would bluster out a few harsh, rude words and then hang up. But one hostile caller was not a stranger. This was an old friend of Konrad's from the army who had been with him during the hardships and victory of the battle of the Baltic Sea. He rang only to call Konrad an enemy of Poland. 'Get out, you Jew!' he said. But far more disturbing and painful to us was silence – the silence of a few friends who had previously been like brothers and sisters to us and who in March suddenly stopped seeing us.

During these difficult days my great support and mainstay was Beata. I now felt overwhelmed with guilt: where had I been when she had suffered? She visited regularly, calling after work on this or that pretext, bringing fruit for the children, coaxing me out for a walk. She seldom talked about what was going on at work, as though to spare me pain. I knew, however, that Ryszard was now boss and was hand in glove with the people who had recently taken over power. I knew that he resented her as much as he hated me. I was very worried she might get into serious trouble for keeping in touch with me, and every time I saw her, I begged her not to come again. Her visits to our place were obviously noted by the spies and so was everything she said. She knew all this but never stopped coming.

More and more often the twins came home from school in tears. Ever since Konrad had been named in Gomułka's speech two boys and a girl in their class had kept calling them Jews. They also said filthy things about their father, and it was more than the girls could bear. They cried but it never lasted long. They were always surrounded by schoolfriends who saw them off after lessons and invited them home.

One day the girls burst into the flat weeping bitterly: a handwritten notice had been stuck up in the lift saying that our family was not to be trusted and should be kicked out of Poland. They were so shocked that they decided to stop using the lift altogether and to climb the stairs instead. Hearing this, I rushed to the landing and called up the lift in order to destroy the offensive message. But when it appeared, someone had already neatly scraped off the piece of paper and only a patch of fresh glue still remained.

The janitor of our big apartment block was an illiterate middle-aged woman who used to do my laundry. I now had lots of time and not enough money so I did it myself. One day she turned up to say she would be happy to do the job for me without pay. She also told us that a priest had been round the flats the day before. He had called on most of our neighbours, she said, telling them that we were decent, honest people worthy of their full respect and support. As we thanked her for the good news, she sighed heavily and said that she had had to keep the priest's visit from her own son, who was 'one of them' and might have denounced both the priest and herself if he had known.

It was like living in a swing boat. From one hour to the next our spirits went up and down, up and down. The nights brought despair and terror.

Near the end of April, in the fourth week of my enforced holiday, I received a letter from the film headquarters: I should report to the Personnel Department on the following day. I went there shaking with anger but did all I could to look cool. A high-ranking official was waiting for me in his sumptuous office. I did not know him well, he had only started at the beginning of the year. In a matter-of-fact way he told me that I must hand in my resignation as there was no work for me in the headquarters. In recognition of my twenty years' service I would receive my salary for the next four – not the statutory three – months. I wrote a brief notice of resignation, signed it and left. Making my way through the corridor I caught a glimpse of the Minister entering his office. He looked aged and wasted.

Later that day, Konrad and I did a simple reckoning. Konrad's salary had stopped on the day of his dismissal. If we were as careful as possible we could live on my salary till the end of August. Then, by using our savings and selling the car, we could keep going for another few months. But what then?

The following days brought more threatening telephone calls.

Five bulky strangers chose a bench in our courtyard and sat there for hours, keeping an eye on the entrance to our staircase and staring straight up into our windows.

Lena came running home, frightened to death: a gang of hooligans had attacked her in the park.

The TV screen was choking with hatred, and spat out Konrad's name time after time.

A scholarly article appeared in a respectable magazine. It attacked Konrad and others for their dangerous influence on Polish youth. It was signed by a close friend.

One night the painful decision was made.

Getting the promise of the Israeli visa from the Dutch embassy was only a matter of hours. From there our way led to the Ministry of the Interior. Within a week we managed to assemble all the documents required and deposit our application for an emigration permit. A time of nerve-racking waiting and uncertainty began.

Applying for permission to go to Israel was the only way of leaving Poland, and the main condition for this was giving up Polish citizenship. For the second time during his reign Gomułka kept his promise and let the Jews go – though only in one direction. By the beginning of May, some people had already been given their travel documents and were about to leave. None of them, however, was so much hated and attacked in the media as Konrad. He was the first person on the black-list to apply. This might be very dangerous. We feared he might be refused a permit once and for all and then separated from me and the children, harassed or even arrested.

Once our decision became known in Warsaw, more people than ever started flocking to our home. Respectable scholars, film-makers, our children's old nannies, friends from the past, friends from the present and complete strangers – all turned up to say how ashamed and sorry they felt that it had to end like this, or to beg us to change our minds.

One afternoon, as we were busy sorting out our huge collection of books trying to decide which to take or leave, we heard heavy panting outside our front door. That day, as so many others, the lift was out of order and someone must have found it hard to climb the stairs. No wonder: it was a frail old lady. She was dressed in dark clothes and wore an old-fashioned wide-rimmed black hat. She held in both her trembling hands an enormous bunch of red roses. She was a well-known senior figure amongst Polish Social Scientists and the widow of a world-famous scholar whose life was a symbol to all of us of the strength and honour of the nation. She sat in one of our uncomfortable armchairs sipping weak tea. She said little, as though the right words were hard to find. But the words did not matter. Just her presence there, an old lady looking so out of date in our modern flat, said more than words could ever express. She did not stay long. But the roses she brought stayed fresh for at least ten days. We knew what she wanted us to know.

Another friend came one day full of indignation to say that he strongly condemned our decision. His eyes burning, his face flushed, he argued that our rightful place was here and that to leave Poland was a betrayal; we should fight the evil like all other honest Poles; our friends would never let us starve. As he carried on like this, the twins came back from school much earlier than usual. They were in a terrible state, shocked and sobbing. During the morning break they had been attacked by a group of children and would certainly have been beaten up had their own classmates not fiercely intervened. Staring at the two miserable figures our indignant friend fell silent. Bewildered and horrified, he soon left, wishing us good luck.

We decided the twins should stop going to school. To brighten up their days, we took them for walks or trips in the car. Wherever we went, wherever we drove we were always followed by a car or a couple of pedestrians. The girls found this funny. From their back seats in the car they would pull faces and poke out their tongues at the men behind. To amuse the children, Konrad would slowly circle a roundabout, over and over again, until we all felt dizzy. Mindlessly, obligingly, the agents would follow suit, round and round again. Once we walked to the Old Town shadowed by a man and a woman who had to get out of their car to go at our pace. We went into a café and ordered coffee for Konrad and myself and cakes for the girls. The couple soon appeared at the door, settled down at the next table and made a lavish order. We drank our coffee in a gulp, told the girls to take their cakes with them, and immediately paid the bill. We left the café just as the waitress was serving the agents massive portions of ice-cream, a pile of cakes and expensive drinks. The man threw a bank note onto the table in exasperation and, leaving all their goodies behind, the couple rushed after us. The girls stopped in the street and waved at them. But what seemed fun in the daylight became terrifying at dusk. Our nights were sleepless.

Friends from school called on our twins every afternoon to tell them what had been going on in lessons that day and what homework they should do. They would take their essays and exercises away and hand them in to their respective teachers on the following day. So the girls were able to keep up with their school work and were never idle. They were often invited out by school and local friends whose parents were happy to have them and sometimes took them out to the country on Sundays themselves. Being twelve and nice-looking, they both had a 'fiancé' of their own age in their class. Monika's was a well-known little horror; Sylvia's was famous as a child star. He had played the main part in a feature film when he was only seven and since then had been now and again given minor parts. One day this boy made an unusual proposal to the twins: the dubbing studio needed some children for the Polish sound-track of a foreign film. He thought that Monika and Sylvia would be ideal. And the studio paid well, he solemnly assured them. Overjoyed, the girls went with him to the studio, worked a day or two and had a lot of fun. They offered us their first-ever earnings to help with their keep. But we said we were not as poor as that yet and they should keep their money. So they went shopping and very sensibly bought themselves some clothes.

Some time later I had a telephone call from the studio. A woman whom I had met only once during my many years in film, said the studio would like to give the twins steady work and pay them regular royalties. Brought almost to tears, I thanked her very warmly but said we would have to think it over. We did still have my salary.

I went to collect my May salary on the last day of the month. Salaries were paid in cash at the beginning or end of each month. I could hardly believe my eyes when I saw the familiar hall that led to my former office. The stylish interior of this once-residential building had changed beyond recognition, the ancient walls were covered with gaudy posters bearing anti-Zionist slogans. One of these posters was glued right on the door of the room where I had previously worked. It said: 'A true Pole has only one Fatherland.'

I was shocked and felt a desperate need to see Beata. I burst into her office, but she was not there. Sitting idly at her desk as usual, Izabella told me that Beata had been transferred to the film warehouse a week earlier. On the day the Minister was sacked, she added. I stared at her in disbelief: Beata had been to see me twice during the last week and had never said a word.

The emigration permit from the Ministry of the Interior came by post on 7 June. It was dated 1 June and was valid till the last day of the month. We had 23 days to go. Both the speed of the response and the closeness of the deadline took us by surprise.

There was no way of asking for an extension, we would just have to move fast.

Konrad, Lena and I went to collect our permits the same day. It did not take long; they seemed to be waiting for us. The clerk who received us had our dossier close at hand. He made a kindly remark about the twins, looking at their photographs pasted next to mine in my travel document, and gave each of us a declaration to sign. We left his office no longer Polish citizens. Nor any other citizens either.

Flowers poured into our home day and night. We often found them waiting at our front door when exhausted and miserable we got back from the city laden with shopping. Time was running short and we had a thousand things to do before we could part with our country and set off into the unknown. Sorting out all the goods and chattels we had accumulated over the years was the most difficult task. We had been ordered to empty the flat before we left and there was very little we could possibly take with us in the car or even squeeze into a large crate we had ordered from a shipping firm. All the furniture had to go, half our huge book collection, most of our clothes. At the same time we still had some savings left that would be of no use abroad. It seemed sensible to spend that money on some new things to replace old ones. So, our minds miles away, we raced from shop to shop randomly buying whatever was available and might be useful in the future. From shop to shop we were followed by the blank-eyed men in civilian clothes.

Among the people who visited us in the evenings was an old friend of mine whom I had not seen for years. Staś had once played an important part in my life – during the Nazi occupation, he had risked his own life to help my family survive. Now in his late fifties, at this far less dangerous but very difficult time, he offered his help again. He took on the job of getting rid of our unwanted belongings, selling them off for us one by one or giving them to people in need. With his help our flat quickly emptied.

Very soon our crate was filled and was delivered to the Customs at Gdansk railway station to be examined before being sealed and shipped to Israel. Konrad and I now had to spend long hours day after day in the heat of the Customs barracks assisting the officials in their searches. We watched helplessly as they ripped open our new quilts and pillows, tore pictures and mirrors from their frames and turned over the leaves of 2,000 books in search of written or typed words which might sap the foundation of their powerful socialist state. There was no end to all this and we feared we might miss the deadline unless we decided to leave the cargo behind.

In the meantime, we lived in an empty flat with only beds, a carpet and a gas cooker. June that year was extremely hot. With no fridge, no proper saucepans and very little free time, we stopped eating at home and went, all five, to a nearby restaurant for lunch. There were piano recitals in this restaurant every Sunday. Once, sitting at lunch and talking about everything we still had to do, we suddenly heard one of Chopin's Nocturnes. An elderly pianist was playing it as if inspired, calling forth all the subtle undertones of that glorious music, painting with the magic sounds a melancholy Polish landscape, telling the story of sufferings with no reprieve and no end. We left our meal unfinished.

Other times, we stopped packing and sank into doubts – when an unknown florist had sent us a huge bouquet of red and white roses; or when a watchmaker refused to take money for repairing our alarm clock. The boat went on swinging.

After eight days in the stuffy barracks the search was finally completed. We were waiting only for a little suitcase which had been taken to the customs office at the beginning of the search to be checked more closely. It contained Konrad's writings – the typescripts of two new books that had been accepted but then returned by the publishers; my many writings from the war; old letters; Konrad's reading notes, sketches, note books; family photographs and other souvenirs that I had always kept. Sealed and strangely light, the suitcase was returned from the Customs office on Friday, 21 June. We had no idea then that they had taken out all our manuscripts. They flung the suitcase onto the top of the tightly packed goods, the crate was immediately sealed and we were free to go. There were now eight days till the deadline. On our way home through the park, followed as usual from a distance, we agreed on a secret date in two whispered words: we did not want the agents to know when we would be leaving, as it could have been dangerous.

That night more people than ever came to see us. Even the empty flat could hardly hold such a crowd, so Lena took her own innumerable friends into the courtyard. In the street at the entrance to our block sinister cars were parked: a dozen secret agents who had followed some of our visitors were now patiently waiting to follow them back home.

In a dazzling heat, our visitors sat on the floor among jars of flowers, leaning against bare walls marked with the pale squares and rectangles where pictures once had hung. Though they knew they were being listened to, that each word was being recorded, they talked for hours about their own and our precarious future. Many friendships were struck between people from different walks of life who had never met before. Adam and Staś poured tepid vodka into some cracked glasses. Pani Waczkowska served ripe cherries and water from the tap. A band of children led by the twins kept wandering in and out from the courtyard, not sure which party to join. In the corridor, Marek and Beata were lost in whispered conversation. My heart leapt when I overheard him offering her a job on his team. I knew what he must have known himself – that he was embarking upon serious trouble.

At midnight our visitors left, some going through the loft and down a distant staircase.

On Saturday we made lots of telephone calls telling everybody we would be leaving on Monday. I phoned the local council and asked them to send someone to collect the apartment keys on Monday morning. In the evening, only three people called on us: a couple of our best friends and Staś. They asked no questions. We begged Staś to come on Monday morning to collect our beds and whatever was still left in the flat, and we gave him our spare keys. Then we kissed our friends more warmly than ever before and they all left.

We sent our girls to bed earlier than usual. Slightly suspicious, they obeyed blindly. At two o'clock the same night we roused them from their sleep. Quickly, softly they got ready without a word. Our bags were already packed. Noiselessly, on tiptoe, we left the flat. In the street our car was waiting alone: there was no sign of the blank-eyed men. In a split second we got in and set off. The streets were deserted, nobody followed us, our plot was successful. We soon left Warsaw behind and made our way along an empty road lined with poplars. The sky over the fields was growing bright. Dawn came.

*

Dawn comes over the Yorkshire moors, with a mild breeze comes the promise of a fine day. Alone under the vast dome of the brightening sky, we walk through the spellbound waste. The light, the scent, the sounds of early morning bring back memories of another life, another country. I left that country in the distant past abandoning all my young hopes and passions. Now I belong nowhere. But perhaps to belong means to love and be loved and this is all that truly matters.